Cook Your Assets

Cook Your Assets

Written by Cindie Haras, CPA
&
Hosted by the Financial Chef

Langdon Street Press
212 3rd Avenue North, Suite 570
Minneapolis, MN 55401
612.455.2293
www.langdonstreetpress.com

ISBN - 978-1-934938-13-3
ISBN - 1-934938-13-0
LCCN - 2008937700

Book sales for North America and international:
Itasca Books, 3501 Highway 100 South, Suite 220
Minneapolis, MN 55416
Phone: 952.345.4488 (toll free 1.800.901.3480)
Fax: 952.920.0541

Cover Design by George Foster www.fostercovers.com
Typeset by James Arneson

Printed in the United States of America

Contents

Acknowledgements

A special thank you to Andy, whose unrelenting support made it possible for his wife to pursue her passion.

To Rich, my conscience, willing me to stay on track and finish this challenge.

To my mom and aunt, the first members of the Cindie Haras Book Club.

To my family, friends, and co-workers who took the book's quizzes. Thank you. Volunteers are hard to find.

And in memory of my dad, you showed me how exciting life can be if I follow my innovative spirit and that ordinary is not for everyone. I share this achievement with you.

Introduction

A bird in the hand is worth two in the bush. A penny saved is a penny earned. Waste not; want not. I think we all have heard one of these expressions during our lifetimes. I frankly have never really understood what these phrases mean. Why is it so desirable to have a bird in your hand anyway? And why can't one save a penny that was given to you? The last one really confuses me. Does it mean if you don't waste anything you'll never want anything or is it that if you don't want anything you'll have nothing to waste? What happened to good old-fashioned simplicity; imagine if everyone would just say what he means and means what he says.

This type of ambiguity and complexity is particularly prevalent in the financial sector. Suppose a genie grants you the wish to receive a dollar for each person who has read and completely comprehended every line of either "War and Peace" or "The Wall Street Journal". My bet is you would choose the classic.

I quote from the the *Wall Street Journal* within its "Money and Investing" section, the following passage. "The argument seems to be that emerging markets are where risk-oriented money goes.... NASDAQ's performance is also viewed as an indicator of investor tolerance for risk. So if appetite for NADAQ risk is down, people reason appetite for emerging market risk is also down." If I didn't know any better, I might have thought this was a quote from a food critic's column rather than an analysis of a stock market trend. I point this out not to malign in any fashion the *Wall Street Journal* for I believe it is a very sophisticated and informative financial newspaper. My purpose is only to demonstrate how the world of finance has its own language, relying on its own dictionary, of which the general population has never received a copy.

Actually, it's unfortunate that financial advice columns can't be more like food critic columns. Let's explore the typical food critic's column. Each has the same basic ingredients: a restaurant, a waiter or waitress, and food. By measuring and mixing these ingredients the food critic formulates his opinion. He may give rave reviews for one place and cast cutting criticism for another. Yet the steps used to reach the determination remain the same. You know from the start, the critic will comment on the establishment's decor, he will judge the quality of service, and he will attest to the chef's culinary abilities. It is a consistent approach.

Now in comparison, let's explore the typical financial advice column. A common person asks for an opinion or answer to a particular financial matter, to which the financial expert displays his expansive knowledge by providing both a cumbersome and complex reply. Usually, the response contains two or three "What if?" scenarios which only serve to confuse the person asking for the advice, to the point of wishing they had never even asked for help.

Thinking about this scenario prompted me to challenge why financial advice cannot be simplified. Why can't technical jargon used by the financial analyst, the certified public accountant, and certified financial planner be translated into a user-friendly vocabulary understood by all?

That's when the concept came to me. What type of book is universally understood? What type of book is the structural outline known before it's even opened by a reader? What type of book has the same fundamental step-by-step approach to its subject matter? The answer is the cookbook.

Is there anyone who at one time or another has not used a cookbook? Why has the cookbook survived for all these generations? My feeling is because its structure and its content have always been consistent and simple. Separated into sections, a cookbook almost always contains appetizer, entrée and dessert segments. When you browse the appetizer section, you're comfortable in knowing you won't find a recipe for Baked Alaska. Structure provides consistency for cookbooks while recipes provide simplicity. What more is a recipe than an outline of steps needed to reach a desired goal . As long as the cook has the basic ingredients needed for the recipe at his disposal, the exercise becomes routine, if not simple. If one follows the recipe's basic steps and uses the required ingredients, one can be almost assured that their dish will turn out as desired. It was with this concept in mind, that I realized financial planning is nothing but a series of steps to reach a desired result, or a recipe with its basic ingredients known. If one can follow and feel comfortable with using a recipe than one can feel comfortable using a recipe to achieve financial goals. Hence, came the origin of this book. Now, here's the question. Why would I want to spend endless hours creating these recipes, drive my husband crazy asking for editorial advice, and subject myself to book reviewers?

The answer is twofold. One reason is I want to challenge the forever attitude that you must be very serious when discussing personal finance. I'm sorry, but seriousness often pairs with boring. So I ask you which is better, teaching with some sarcastic humor or teaching to an absent audience? People already have enough severe issues to deal with. Just watch the TV news; that's enough to sober anyone up. I know money is a serious business, but often people can identify and learn better when humor is injected into the lesson. Also, I'm objecting to the stereotype that all accountants are boring. We're not! Okay, I have to admit, some accountants are unbelievably dull and void of personalities. I've had to work with them, but, I repeat , some!

The other reason for writing this recipe book is to help those who are too intimidated to learn more about money and personal finance issues. I started my certified public accounting practice twenty years ago when I was 26 years old. Wow, damn I'm old!

My dad's small business was one of my first clients. True story. I purchased this fancy software program to enter my clients' financial activities. I input my dad's information into the program and produced this fancy monthly report. I met with my father and handed him this detailed financial statement. He looked at it and handed it back to me saying, "What the hell am I supposed to do with that!" Crushed, I said, "This is your blah-blah report citing a bunch of technical terms. You need to know this." He looked at me, and said, "No, you need to know this. You're just providing me with a report stating all the things you know. All accountants do this. You produce all these complicated statements to show us that you know something. Well, here's what I need to know. I want to see what my sales were for the month, what it cost to produce those sales and what my salaries were. It's that simple. If you want to still produce this report for yourself, well fine, but don't give it to me."

I still carry this lesson with me today. Speak to people in a voice they can understand. Teach people what they need to know instead of what you know.

Keep it as simple as possible and people will benefit more.

I was in my office, meeting with a tax client. Her husband had passed away that year. She was practically in tears, apologizing that she didn't know what she was to have brought to our meeting. "My husband always took care of the taxes. I feel so lost, I don't even know how to write a check" she explained.

I truly felt bad for this woman. She had relied on her husband to take care of all their financial matters. Unfortunately, he never planned for how she would cope when he was gone. I thought about recommending a personal finance book to her, but realized I couldn't think of one that would cover the basics and speak to her in a voice she could understand.

Throughout my career, I have talked with many people with similar experiences. Giving someone a starting point and the confidence to change their situation is my goal. Stress results from not knowing how to achieve financial goals. Some of us purchase financial planning books and are disillusioned because the books are too difficult to understand. This book addresses the basics, and provides people with a starting point.

Section I

Essentials
to Stock Your Pantry
❦

Suppose on your way home from work each night you stop by the grocery store. Whether for an essential ingredient to that night's recipe or just the usual milk, soda or bread, you still stop. At best, each trip consumes 15 minutes from your already overbooked schedule. After one year you will have wasted nearly 80 hours. That's the equivalent to a two-week vacation from work. I don't know about you, but I have never wanted to vacation in the canned goods aisle of the grocery store.

Saving time is not the only reason to keep your pantry properly stocked; so is saving dollars. How many times on your way home from work have you darted into a convenience store with only five minutes to spare before guests are to arrive for your dinner party. This time, coffee is the missing staple from your pantry. You grab a dwarf size container, housing eight whole ounces of ground coffee, from the dusty shelf only to be utterly appalled at the $ 6.99 price tag. Lesson to be learned; every efficient cook keeps a well-stocked pantry.

The same holds true for financial planning. The only difference is the types of items the financial planning and cooking pantries store. Below is a list of items every financial planning pantry should contain along with their relative shelf life. Shelf life, in this case, refers to the frequency to which the item should be reviewed for modifications and updates.

How many of the following items are in your financial pantry right now? Your answer will determine just how much shopping will be necessary. Actually, some of the above ingredients may be foreign to you right now. After browsing the list, you might have asked, "What's a revocable living trust and where do I buy one?" In this book's remaining sections you will learn what these ingredients are, how they are used in "Personal Finance Recipes" and where to find them.

Financial Planning Pantry	Related Shelf Life
Bank Accounts	One year
Tax Returns	One year
Insurance policies	Earlier of One Year or After Major Life Purchase or Event
Stocks, Bonds, Other Investment Securities	At least Quarterly (3 months)
Last Will and Testament	One Year or After Significant Life Changing Event
Durable Power of Attorney	One Year or After Significant Life Changing Event
Revocable Living Trust	One Year
IRA (Retirement Plans)	One Year
Safe Deposit Box	One Year
Household Budget	One Month

Section II

Menu Planner

See if this scenario is familiar. You are driving home from work after a really stressful day. With your favorite CD in the car stereo, your mind starts to finally slip into a catatonic state. Just about the time when all of the stress of the day has vanished , your cellular phone rings. As customary, you look at your caller ID even though you already know who has disrupted your tranquility. "No, No, I hadn't really thought about it yet", you hear yourself saying. This is the routine reply you make when asked the question, "What do you want to have for dinner tonight".

Every evening, your drive home includes this dinner debate. The debate topics include Italian versus Mexican, or chicken versus fish, or take-out versus leftovers. After a few minutes of playing the "Who-Wants-What" game, the decision of steaks on the grill is made. You hang up the phone feeling worn out but at least now you have a plan of action. Turning the music back on, your mind starts to slip back to that blissful catatonic state.

Sound familiar? I would venture to say, everyone has participated in these dinner debates at one time or another, with some engaging more often than others. What really just happened here though? The answer is a menu was planned. You may ask, "Why bother planning a menu? Is it really necessary?" The answer to these questions requires you to remember back to a time when you didn't go through this process. What happened then? Most likely, someone was left hungry because they couldn't or wouldn't eat what was being served. Discovering everyone's likes and dislikes ahead of time will reduce this risk. The end result is a positive outcome.

Financial planning starts with the same process. Your financial plan is a menu of goals. Your individual likes and dislikes determine the goals you set for yourself. The resources available to you shape these goals. Therefore, the first step in the process is to determine your financial likes and dislikes. The next step is to confirm the existing resources you already have. Both of these steps will be accomplished through the use of worksheets called financial fact finders. When completing the financial fact finders, please be aware that there are no wrong answers, so be as honest as possible.

Money Mentality Fact Finder

Of the following ten (10) questions , select the answer that is nearest to your personal situation or preference.

1. Your goals about money are:

a. *to spend for todaybecause you never know what may happen tomorrow.*
b. *to save every extra penny because the golden years will come sooner than you think.*
c. *to spend for the basics and give in to an occasional impulse buy.*
d. *to have enough to make certain that you can buy whatever you want.*

2. Your great Aunt Agnes, five generations removed, passes on. Unexpectedly, you are summoned to the reading of the will. Poor Aunt Agnes, to be taken so early in life; after all, she was only ninety-seven year old. Your grief is softened after you learn dear old Aunt Agnes has willed $ 100,000.00 of her little nest egg to you. Your first impulse is to:

a. *buy that exotic sports car with the real Italian leather. Aunt Agnes would have wanted you to be happy.*
b. *put the money into a ten-year certificate of deposit. Ten years from now, you'll be glad you were so sensible.*
c. *splurge a little and book that Caribbean cruise you've been fantasizing about. You invest the remaining balance of your windfall in a solid mutual fund.*
d. *use the money to make a down payment on a new home in the affluent section of town. Sure, your mortgage will be more now, but you have thirty years to pay it off.*

3. Your opinion of the value of money in your life is that:

a. *money is very important. You need it to drive your fantasies. Without money, life would be ordinary.*

b. *you worry about money. Holding on to money guarantees your well being.*

c. *you try not to be obsessive about money. If you live modestly, money should take care of itself.*

d. *it seems that as soon as you start getting ahead, some new bill sets you back.*

4. A budget is:

a. *a curse word. You prefer to think of a flexible spending plan.*

b. *okay for some, but you don't have to follow a plan to be the watchdog of you nest egg.*

c. *necessary. Without one, you may succumb to the occasional impulse buy.*

d. *a work of fiction. You have a hard enough time keeping your head above water.*

5. You receive in the mail a pre-approved credit card application guaranteeing $25,000.00, you:

a. *complete it. If approved, you can invest the money in that new dot-com stock a friend told you of and double your investment.*

b. *tear it up; as much as possible you avoid credit.*

c. *analyze the terms offered; perhaps, you could consolidate all your cards into one payment and save a few dollars.*

d. *complete it; you have past due bills that need attention.*

6. A group of your co-workers have decided to branch off and start their own company. They ask you to be part of the group. The venture is risky, but if everything goes according to plan, you could be making ten times as much money in a couple of years. You:

a. *take the risk and join the new endeavor. If the business fails, you can always find another job.*

b. *decline their offer. You've invested too much time where you're at to take the chance.*

c. *stick it out where you are, perhaps, you'll get a promotion and raise after your co-workers have moved on.*

d. *accept the opportunity. You're living above your means right now and need to find a way to get back on an even keel.*

7. As far as saving money is concerned, you:

a. *Don't really worry about it; after all, one of your investments will make a significant return soon.*
b. *Were born to save;, you're always looking for new ways to set aside more money.*
c. *have difficulty saving money which bothers you at times.*
d. *have more immediage financial concerns.*

8. When it comes to debt, you:

a. *believe someday you will be debt free.*
b. *wonder how some people let themselves become so far in debt that they have to declare bankruptcy to recover.*
c. *are willing to borrow for emergencies; however, you often have a difficult time differentiating what is and isn't an emergency.*
d. *don't really know at any one given point in time how much you owe.*

9. Which of the following options would you most desire?

a. *$ 20,000.00 cash today to invest any way you want, but in ten years you would have to pay $15,000.00 of the cash back. Access to the money would be limited to investment purposes only.*
b. *$10,000.00 today, but the cash must be held in a money market account for five years before you are allowed to lay a hand on it.*
c. *$10,000.00 today, to invest anyway you want, but you must pay seven percent interest on the cash for five years. Access to the money would be limited to investment purposes only.*
d. *$5,000.00 today to spend in any fashion you want.*

10. Which of the following options would be least desirable:

a. *$5,000.00 in cash*
b. *10,0000 shares of "double your money"dot-com stock, currently*

valued at $10,000, but you would have to hold the stock for six months before you could sell it.

c. *A collectible piece of artwork, currently appraised at $5,000.00.*

d. *$10,000.00 contribution to a retirement plan, whose benefits are payable only when you reach retirement.*

Risky Rick   Conservative Carla   Moderate Melvin   Debtor Debbie

Based upon your answers to the money mentality questions, you will fall into one of the above four personality types.

If your responses were mostly "a", you are a Risky Rick.
Likely character traits:
- plays the lottery on a regular basis
- lives more for today than worry about tomorrow
- is content with sometimes having to start over
- does not have an emergency fund
- feels his investments will be able to fund his retirement
- has entrepreneurial spirit
- files his taxes, but often needs an extension

If your responses were mostly "b", you are a Conservative Clara.
Likely character traits:
- funds her retirement plan fully
- carries full health insurance coverage
- knows at any given time how much she has in savings
- is rigid in thinking, unreceptive to new ideas and situations
- does not seek professional financial advice or guidance
- files her taxes promptly

If your responses were mostly "c", you are a Moderate Melvin.
Likely character traits:
- depends on the advise of professional financial consultants
- files his taxes on time, often using a tax preparer
- works for a sizable corporation or company
- worries about how he will fund his retirement

If your responses were mostly "d", you are a Debtor Debbie.
Likely character traits:
- lives paycheck to paycheck
- acts impulsively
- acts as if unaccountable for her actions
- is transient in nature, whether in terms of a job or their place to live

What are you really worth? Ask people this question and most will have some kind of answer. Some individuals will use their bank balance to state their personal worth. Others will go a step further and include the value of their home and their car. Others will only focus on their debt and offer a disgusted cursory response of "not a dime". A few may ask an insightful, yet morbid question, "Would that be my worth if I was dead or alive?" before responding.

No matter what the reply, each person's reasoning used in determining an amount will differ. Lets go back to Debtor Debbie, Risky Rick, Moderate Melvin & Conservative Clara and think about how each would answer this question. Their grasp on net worth most likely will follow their money mentality.

For instance, Debtor Debbie would be likely to ignore her credit card debt when figuring her personal wealth. She thinks, "Why should I count that? I'm making the minimum payments each month." Never mind that she owes more than $ 15,000.00 on her Bloomingdale's card and that by making only the minimum payment each month, she could be eighty-five by the time she pays off the balance.

Now, Risky Rick is a different story. He measures the value of items for their future worth not for their present value. You might wonder what that means? For example, Risky Rick is riding the subway, to work one day, when he overhears two white-collar executives discussing their purchase of a blue chip stock that has been undervalued by the financial world. They have ironclad information that the stock is set for a huge upward jump. Its price is $45 and is a sure bet to double in the next year. Risky Rick, a gambler at heart, looks at the opportunity as a sure thing and gobbles up 200 shares for himself. Ask him what his net worth is, and his reply will include the value of his new hot stock at the projected future price, determined by a couple stuffed shirt executives. Dangerous money mentality, especially since the stock was Enron Corporation, now one of the largest U.S. corporate collapses ever. Ouch!

Let's leap forward a bit. You determine your net worth to be $1,000.00. "Wow!" you think that's pitiful! "I should be screaming for a financial makeover." This would be true if you are 65 years old. But what if you are 18 years old and a college student? See where this is going? First, you need to arrive at an amount, but that by itself is not enough. You still haven't determined if you're climbing the ladder fast enough. Should you be one or two rungs higher at your age? Should you be one or two rungs higher with your particular personal status? The answers may surprise you. Take the financial footing fact finder to see where you are. Please select the answer closest to your circumstances.

Financial Footing Fact Finder

1. Your age is:

a. under 25.
b. 25 to 39 years old.
c. 40 to 65 years old.
d. 65 and above.

2. Your cash savings are:

a. zero.
b. less than $ 5,000.
c. greater than $ 5,000.
d. overdrawn in your checking account in the past six months.

3. Your current home status is:

a. you are renting.
b. you own your own home and pay a mortgage.
c. you own your own home and pay a mortgage and mortgage insurance.
d. you own your own home mortgage free.

4. With respect to life insurance:

a. you have no life insurance and no debt.
b. you have no life insurance and have debt.
c. you have term life insurance.
d. you have level term life insurance that is held in a trust.

5. With respect to your children:
a. you have no children.
b. you have enrolled in your state's prepaid college program.
c. you have not made any real provisions for your child's education.
d. you have both enrolled in your state's prepaid college education and contribute each year to an educational IRA account.

6. With respect to your retirements savings:

a. you participate in your company's retirement plan.
b. You do not have an employer provided retirement plan, but you contribute to your own IRA account.
c. you don't save any real money for retirement.
d. you're already retired and are withdrawing your funds.

7. With respect to debt:

a. you make an extra mortgage payment each month.
b. you only pay the minimum payments for your credit cards.
c. you hold a mortgage whose term is 15 years, not 30 .
d. you have credit cards but try to pay the entire balance each month.

8. In order to retire comfortably, you anticipate you will need how much in savings?

a. One year of your current earnings
b. None, social security will be enough.
c. Enough to pay you at least 80% of your final year's salary each year.
d. None, your kids will take care of you.

9. With respect to long-term care insurance, you:

a. are currently paying policy premiums.
b. are receiving benefits under a policy.
c. are under the age of forty.
d. have no long-term insurance. You have lots of relatives who will be more than happy to wipe the drool from your mouth.

10. With respect to disability insurance, you:

a. have a policy that will provide benefits for you while you are disabled.
b. have no coverage, you don't get sick?
c. have no coverage, you have health insurance.
d. have minimal coverage provided by your employer.

Answers

1. a = 20	2. a = 0	3. a = 0	4. a = 0	5. a = 0
b = 10	b = 10	b = 10	b = -10	b = 10
c = 0	c = 20	c = -10	c = 10	c = -10
d = -10	d = -10	d = 20	d = 20	d = 20

6. a = 20	7. a = 20	8. a = 10	9. a = 10	10. a = 20
b = 10	b = -10	b = 0	b = 20	b = -10
c = 0	c = 10	c = 20	c = 0	c = 0
d = -10	d = 0	d = -10	d = -10	d = 20

IF YOU SCORED BETWEEN "0 & 100"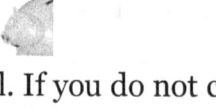

You have along way before you piggy bank is full. If you do not change your habits now, you will be in financial trouble in the golden years. It takes time to save a nest egg. Any extra effort towards saving money either in the short time or long term will improve your situation.

IF YOU SCORED BETWEEN "1 & 100"

Your piggy bank is starting to take some real shape. You may need to devote some energy towards less commonplace retirement strategies such as long-term health insurance or disability insurance policies.

IF YOU SCORED GREATER THAN "100"

Your piggy bank is a potbelly full. You have taken steps to ready yourself for retirement. Continue along the same path you have been on. You should make a continuous effort to keep current of new tax laws, financial products and movements in the economy. Make sure your investment portfolio stays flexible so that changes can be made as trends in the market place change.

Each of the *Cook Your Assets* recipes has certain items in common. The next section is the financial recipe guide.

Each recipe presented uses chef hats to signify the financial recipe's degree of difficulty.

= Simple or Basic -Minimal Preparation Time.

= Moderately Complicated – Average Preparation Time

= Complex – Considerable Preparation Time

= Best Prepared By a Professional

Each recipe contains a chart displaying the financial recipe's nutritional value. The nutritional value is broken down into the following categories:

- **Risk**
- **Long Term Value or Growth Potential**
- **Income Producing**
- **Tax Savings**

These nutritional chart factors are scored between zero and one hund-red with zero being a low value and one hundred being a high value.

For example, a score of 90 for the risk factor means the asset that is rather high in risk. A score of 20 for long-term value or growth potential means the asset is low in growth potential or long term pay off. An asset that is income producing will score high if it generates cash flow. A stock that pays a large quarterly dividend would score close to one hundred for income producing factor. The tax savings factor would score high for those assets that produce tax savings or are tax-free.

The financial recipe's nutritional value chart is a guideline to help you assess the strength and weaknesses of the particular personal finance recipe. It is not a guarantee. Specific assets may differ from those we will discuss.

Each recipe also has a guest appearance of the Financial Chef.

The Financial Chef is non-sexual but I'll use the pronoun "He" because it's one less letter to type. His job is to provide a quick tidbit of information regarding the recipe. He, along with a little help from me, created all these great recipes. He also shows up in the cookbook when he thinks I need a little help expressing myself. Then there are just times he just appears because he wants attention.

Section III

Appetizers
For the Early Years

৩ ৶

Webster's Dictionary defines an appetizer as a small portion of food or drink served at the beginning of a meal to stimulate the appetite. In definitive terms, an appetizer is the starter course that sets the stage for the rest of the meal.

Have you ever been to a friend's house for dinner and served an appetizer not fit for your dog's consumption? What crossed your mind at the time? Most likely, you formulated a notion that the remainder of the meal would be just as dreadful if not worse. In contrast, if the appetizer is outstanding then your appetite is stimulated for the remainder of the meal. The appetizer unknowingly can make or break the meal's success. The same concept holds true for personal finance. In order to have a successful financial plan, certain preliminary steps need to be taken.

Financial planning appetizers are the starters for the main course. These recipes establish the basics in financial planning. Establishing certain fundamentals early in life will set the stage for making intelligent investment decisions in later years. The financial planning process becomes second nature. With practice, what was once taxing becomes relaxing. Don't confuse routine with stagnant though. The economy is continuously changing and evolving. New financial products are introduced to meet these changes. Evaluating these products will be easier for you because you will already have a basis of experience to draw from.

Checking Accounts with Crispy Cash
"Open a Checking Account"

Don't forget to deduct those Debit Card and ATM transactions from your checking account balance! Many banks charge as high as a $35 fee for an overdraft on your account. So a $10 ATM transaction could end up costing you another $35!

There are several different types of checking accounts. Interest rates, check writing limits, minimum balances, and ATM transactions offered are a few of the distinguishing characteristics of checking accounts. On-line banking is extremely popular. I think this feature is great because it keeps you honest. If you view your account activity regularly, you'll be aware of transactions you may have forgotten to record.

Checking Accounts with Crispy Cash
"Open a Checking Account"

Ingredients

Bank, credit union or brokerage house

Money for the initial deposit

Driver's license for proof of I.D

Social security card

Preparation

1. Take ingredients to either bank, credit union or brokerage house. Ask one of the bank tellers to direct you to someone who handles new accounts.

2. Inform the new account rep that you would like to open a personal checking account.

3. Choose additional options for your new checking account

   ATM card

   Debit card

   On-Line Access and Bill Paying Features

   Overdraft Protection

4. Provide the money for the initial deposit

5. Request copies of all forms you have signed

6. Reconcile your check book every month!

Recipe's Financial Nutritional Value
10=Degree of Risk
10=Long Tem Value or Growth Potential
10=Income Producing
0 =Tax Savings

Sample Bank Statement

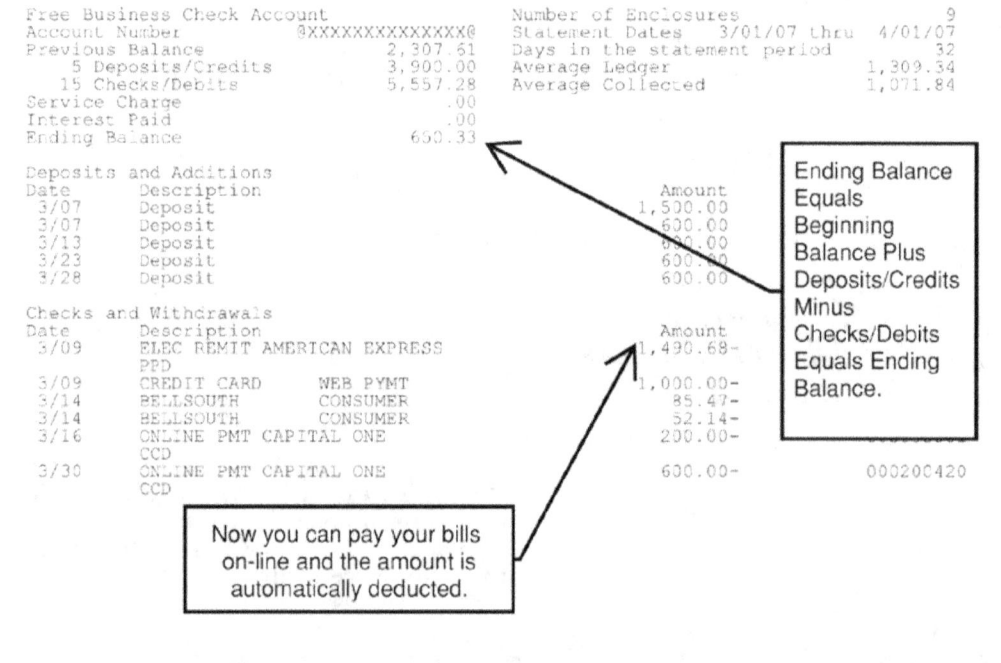

ABC Bank
123 Banking Street
Hometown, USA 99999

Account # 0001-001-0022

The Financial Chef
123 Main Street
Hometown, USA 99999

Date 3/30/07   Page   1
Primary   @XXXXXXXXXXXXXX@

CIF#   H44321

Checking Account
The Financial Chef

Account Title:

    Need a new car, boat or just want to remodel your home?
    Visit our friendly Consumer Loan Specialists for more
    details.

Free Business Check Account   Number of Enclosures   9
Account Number   @XXXXXXXXXXXXXX@ Statement Dates 3/01/07 thru 4/01/07
Previous Balance   2,307.61   Days in the statement period   32
    5 Deposits/Credits   3,900.00   Average Ledger   1,309.34
   15 Checks/Debits   5,557.28   Average Collected   1,071.84
Service Charge   .00
Interest Paid   .00
Ending Balance   650.33

Deposits and Additions
Date   Description   Amount
3/07   Deposit   1,500.00
3/07   Deposit   600.00
3/13   Deposit   600.00
3/23   Deposit   600.00
3/28   Deposit   600.00

Checks and Withdrawals
Date   Description   Amount
3/09   ELEC REMIT AMERICAN EXPRESS   1,490.68-
          PPD
3/09   CREDIT CARD   WEB PYMT   1,000.00-
3/14   BELLSOUTH   CONSUMER   85.47-
3/14   BELLSOUTH   CONSUMER   52.14-
3/16   ONLINE PMT CAPITAL ONE   200.00-
          CCD
3/30   ONLINE PMT CAPITAL ONE   600.00-   000200420
          CCD

Ending Balance
Equals
Beginning
Balance Plus
Deposits/Credits
Minus
Checks/Debits
Equals Ending
Balance.

Now you can pay your bills
on-line and the amount is
automatically deducted.

ABC Bank
123 Banking Street
Hometown, USA 99999

The Financial Chef
123 Main Street
Hometown, USA 99999

Date 3/30/07   Page   2

Account # 0001-001-0022

Free Business Check Account   @XXXXXXXXXXXXXXX@   (Continued)

Checks in Number Order

3/13	1580 (	500.00	0C1731345	3/16	1582*	84.55	000834023
3/15	1588*	15.75	0C0718848	3/12	1589	15.00	001122804
3/16	1590	510.19	003709776	3/13	1591	50.00	000280443
3/16	1621*	400.00	0C0834020	3/13	1622	500.00	002032225
3/06	16	53.50	002335620				

*Denotes missing check numbers

* * *   E N D   O F   S T A T E M E N T   * * *

The asterick is helpful in
identifying outstanding checks.

Let's Get Some More Info for Opening a Bank Account...

What are your options?

ATM versus Debit Card

ATM cards allow you to withdraw cash, pay credit card bills, receive cash advances on credit cards, check your account balances and make deposits. Debit cards afford the same services. Debit card users can also use their card to purchase items in retail stores. When the card is scanned by the retailer, the user's account is automatically reduced. Retailers are happy because they receive the cash almost instantaneously. Per transaction fees charged by retailers and lack of float time for your transaction are drawbacks to debit cards. The choice is a matter of personal preference.

Online Access

Online access is becoming increasingly popular. Most checking accounts can be accessed online today, so you can view your account transactions at anytime. Want to know if your deposit cleared? What to know if you bounced a check? Forget to record that debit card purchase? Just enter your Personal Identification Number (PIN), and both current and previous activity can be viewed. Take the technology one step further, and you can set up your bank to pay your bills automatically. The whole process may seem overwhelming at first, but after a few months, you will wonder how you ever did without this convenience.

Overdraft Protection

Have you ever bounced a check? Almost everyone has at one time or another. No matter how careful we try to be, that pesky forgotten check falls through the cracks, wreaking havoc on the rest of our checking account transactions. At the current rate of about $ 28.00 per bounced check, it doesn't take long before an innocent oversight becomes a costly nightmare. Get overdraft protection and leave this worry behind. The overdraft is covered automatically from a credit card, savings account or special line of credit.

Congratulations, you've cooked an asset!

Here's a financial diet tip!

Watch out for Retail Therapy!

Beware of the signs. Are you going through a life changing event? Often, we use retail therapy to help us feel better. Just like overeating or overindulging in anything, the relief that is felt is often short lived. Make sure you are honest with yourself about your spending habits! What may start out as a temporary behavior becomes a learned response. Don't be Pavlov's dog!

Creamy Credit Card Chipolte Dip
"Applying for a Credit Card"

Watch out for sneaky credit card company practices. Read the pages that follow to become aware of credit card scams!

If someone paid you a dime for every credit card application you receive in the mail each day, you would be so rich you wouldn't even need a credit card! Well, actually you still would because there are some things you just can't purchase or do, without using that little plastic card. A credit card, not cash, allows one to purchase your favorite Jimmy Choo shoes from the internet.

Creamy Chipolte Credit Card Dip
"Applying for a Credit Card"

Analyze your credit. Do you have positive or negative credit history?

***If You Have Good Credit ***

Ingredients

Credit card company

Security deposit (if an unsecured card)

Credit card application — either by mail, by internet or your local bank

Social security number

Preparation

1. Use the internet to look for best options available. Some websites to view –cardweb.com, creditcard.com and creditcardmenu.com—all provide the latest offerings of credit card companies

2. Look for no annual fees, zero or low Introductory APR (interest rate charged on your balance).

3. Look for Reward Programs— that actually give you money back or gifts for using your card more.

4. Complete the credit application. Don't miss reporting any income sources ie: alimony, part time work, interest income. Also, note on the credit application if you are transferring any credit card balances.

5. Check your monthly statement for errors!

Recipe's Financial Nutritional Value
10=Degree of Risk
10=Long Tem Value or Growth Potential
10=Income Producing
0 =Tax Savings

Creamy Chipolte Credit Card Dip
"Applying for a Credit Card"

Analyze your credit. Do you have positive or negative credit history?

***If You Have Bad or No Credit ***

Ingredients

Credit card company

Security deposit (if an unsecured card)

Credit card application – either by mail, by internet or your local bank

Social security number

Preparation

1. Try applying for a credit card with a major department store. Retailers always want to increase their sales, providing shoppers with a credit card is one way to do so.

2. Try your bank. If you aren't a bounced check offender, your bank may be willing to take a risk on you.

3. Try searching online for companies offering secured credit cards. A secured credit card requires the cardholder to provide a deposit or down payment which the cardholder is allowed to borrow against.

4. Complete the application. Be careful submitting information containing your social security number. If online, make sure the site is secure. If by mail, try to send by Fed Ex to a specific person's attention.

5 PAY YOUR NEW CREDIT CARD BILL ON TIME!

Recipe's Financial Nutritional Value
10=Degree of Risk
10=Long Tem Value or Growth Potential
10=Income Producing
0 =Tax Savings

Sample Credit Card Statement

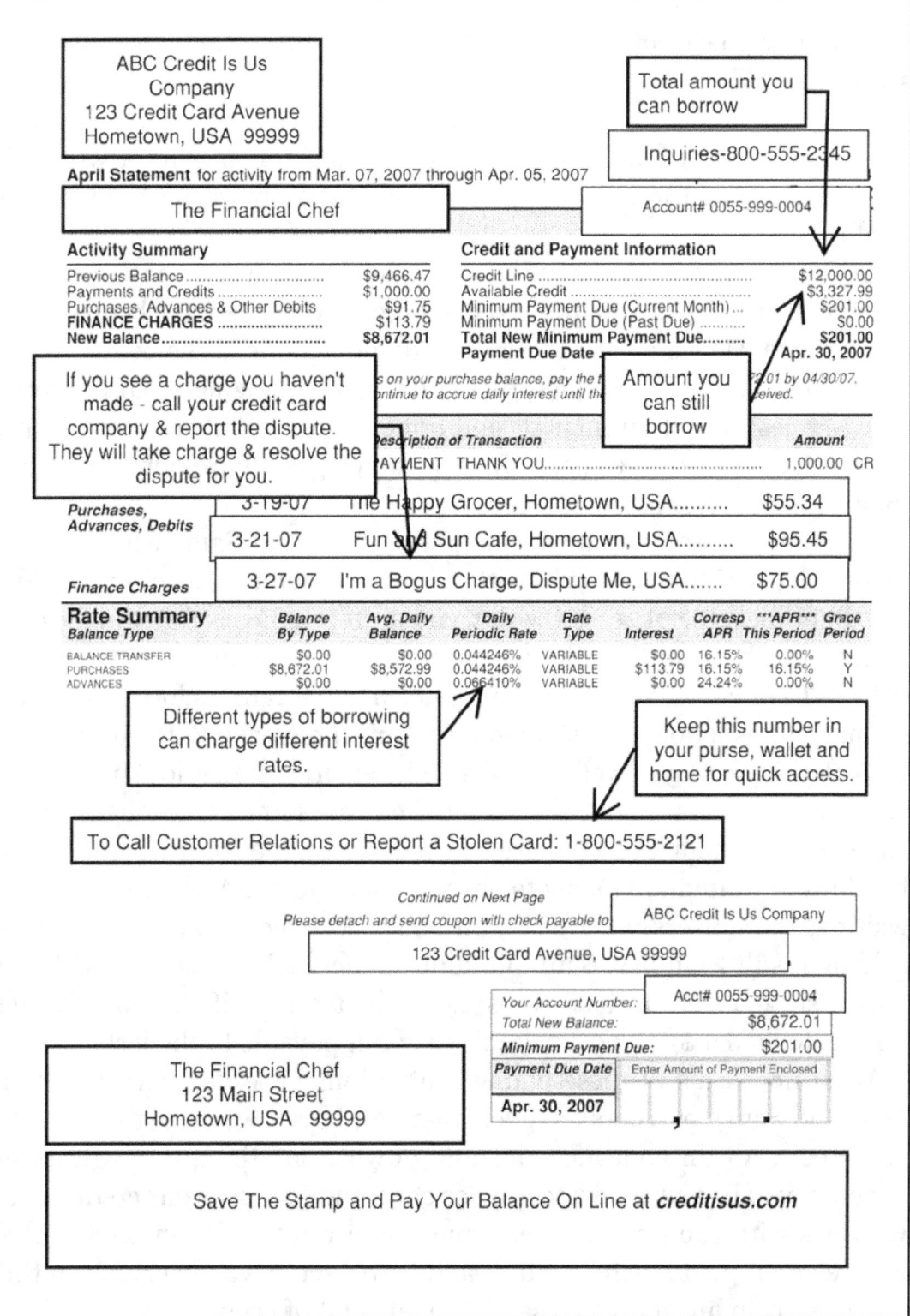

ABC Credit Is Us
Company
123 Credit Card Avenue
Hometown, USA 99999

Total amount you can borrow

Inquiries-800-555-2345

April Statement for activity from Mar. 07, 2007 through Apr. 05, 2007

The Financial Chef

Account# 0055-999-0004

Activity Summary

Previous Balance	$9,466.47
Payments and Credits	$1,000.00
Purchases, Advances & Other Debits	$91.75
FINANCE CHARGES	$113.79
New Balance	$8,672.01

Credit and Payment Information

Credit Line	$12,000.00
Available Credit	$3,327.99
Minimum Payment Due (Current Month)	$201.00
Minimum Payment Due (Past Due)	$0.00
Total New Minimum Payment Due	$201.00
Payment Due Date	Apr. 30, 2007

If you see a charge you haven't made - call your credit card company & report the dispute. They will take charge & resolve the dispute for you.

Amount you can still borrow

...s on your purchase balance, pay the f... ...01 by 04/30/07.
...ntinue to accrue daily interest until th... ...ceived.

	Description of Transaction	Amount
	PAYMENT THANK YOU	1,000.00 CR

Purchases, Advances, Debits

3-19-07	The Happy Grocer, Hometown, USA	$55.34
3-21-07	Fun and Sun Cafe, Hometown, USA	$95.45

Finance Charges

3-27-07	I'm a Bogus Charge, Dispute Me, USA	$75.00

Rate Summary

Balance Type	Balance By Type	Avg. Daily Balance	Daily Periodic Rate	Rate Type	Interest	Corresp APR	***APR*** This Period	Grace Period
BALANCE TRANSFER	$0.00	$0.00	0.044246%	VARIABLE	$0.00	16.15%	0.00%	N
PURCHASES	$8,672.01	$8,572.99	0.044246%	VARIABLE	$113.79	16.15%	16.15%	Y
ADVANCES	$0.00	$0.00	0.066410%	VARIABLE	$0.00	24.24%	0.00%	N

Different types of borrowing can charge different interest rates.

Keep this number in your purse, wallet and home for quick access.

To Call Customer Relations or Report a Stolen Card: 1-800-555-2121

Continued on Next Page

Please detach and send coupon with check payable to

ABC Credit Is Us Company

123 Credit Card Avenue, USA 99999

Your Account Number:	Acct# 0055-999-0004
Total New Balance:	$8,672.01
Minimum Payment Due:	$201.00
Payment Due Date	Enter Amount of Payment Enclosed
Apr. 30, 2007	

The Financial Chef
123 Main Street
Hometown, USA 99999

Save The Stamp and Pay Your Balance On Line at *creditisus.com*

Let's Get Some More Info for Applying for a Credit Card...

Julie was married. "Was" being the key word. Her lousy cheating spouse moved on, leaving her with definite debt issues. Julie has fallen behind on her monthly payments. Worse, her ex-husband had cancelled her Visa credit card and applied for a new card for the "other woman". Julie had owned the card jointly but unfortunately wasn't the primary cardholder.

Oh, almost forgot to mention... her husband, when they were still together, had convinced Julie to book a cruise to the Caribbean on her MasterCard. He called the trip a second honeymoon. Julie believed that it was to be their second honeymoon, she never imagined that he would take her best friend on their second honeymoon! While he was sipping margaritas on the upper deck, Julie was trying to figure out how to pay for a $ 5,000.00 cruise.

Okay, guys, women can be dreadful too. Take Sam, whose newly divorced also. He fell in love with Betsy at nineteen. Reaching middle age, Betsy became obsessed with trying to retain her youth. She begged Sam to give her a million dollar makeover for Christmas. Well, actually the total bill was $ 34,599.00, an a la carte bargain including hip and stomach liposuction, breast augmentation, and eleven Botox injections. By Valentine's Day, swelling subsided, leaving Betsy looking fifteen years younger. Sam thought she looked awesome. He bought her a super-sized bouquet of red roses on the way home from work. He and his flowers waited anxiously for her to come home. After three days of waiting, the flowers were dead, and Sam realized Betsy had left him. Adding insult to injury, Sam found out Betsy had shacked up with her plastic surgeon. Sam was furious; not only had his wife left him for her doctor, he had a $34,599.00 credit card bill payable to the jerk!

What does each of these pathetic situations have in common? Both Julie and Sam's partners have left them and even worse left them with bad credit. All through life's ups and downs, one thing that will never abandon you is your credit score. For good and for bad, your credit score will stick with you forever. Treat your credit right and your credit score will be good to you. Screw with it and it will screw you back. Learn this lesson early in life and you'll save yourself a lot of grief.

So how is your credit rating? Do you have a positive or negative credit history? Or perhaps you have no credit history at all. Determining your credit status will establish what credit card options are available to you. Two terms often used are "Super Prime" and "Sub-Prime" referring to those with excellent credit standing and those with below average credit. Don't know what your credit record is? The internet offers many options to request a credit report. Caution should be used in choosing which internet site you use to obtain this information. Make sure the site is security-protected. Our next recipe "Analyzing Your Credit Report" helps you obtain your credit information.

With credit rating info in hand, you're ready to shop credit card companies.

All credit card companies are not created equal. Watch out for sneaky credit card company practices. Some credit card companies assess hidden fees and rate increases that you may not have bargained for. Here are a few to keep your eyes open to:

 Watch for "Fixed Rates" that do not stay fixed. Only fifteen days notice is required before a credit card company can increase your rates. What's worse the increase does not have to be justified. Only during the grace period are interest rates fixed.

 Don't get hooked into credit card theft insurance. If your card is stolen, Federal law limits your liability to $50.

 Watch out for the unexpected fees charged with balance transfers. You may be quoted a low interest rate (APR) but be careful for additional fees charged on the transfer.

 Don't be late with a payment. Credit card companies are raising their fees for late payments. For proof of payment, most credit card companies offer paying your balance online. Confirmation of payment date and time are available for print and usable for any future discrepancies.

 Don't exceed your credit limit. Not only is this a negative for your credit report, many credit card companies will assess an over the limit fee for charges exceeding your maximum allowance.

 Don't fall for those teaser rates. Zero percent financing can only last so long. The follow- up rate may make you cringe.

 Need a cash advance? Use your ATM card. Credit card companies not only charge interest on the cash advance but also levy a fee as a percentage, usually from 2-4%, of the transaction.

These are some of the traps that credit card companies want you to fall into. Applying for a credit card is definitely one of those times when you want to read the fine print.

On a positive note, be sure to check out whether your credit card company offers any rewards programs. Rewards programs are gaining popularity with credit card companies. Credit card companies actually give you money back or gifts for using your card more. What a concept! Spend money to get money! Now, this is not a license to go out and charge up a storm so that you can get a new mp3 player. You'll still be left with the credit card debt. All rewards programs are not created equal either. You may want to review each card's program before applying for your card. Programs can focus on cash, travel, or retail rewards.

Congratulations, you've cooked another asset!

Here's a financial diet tip!

If you are in good standing with your credit card company, try asking them to lower your interest rate. You'd be surprised how often they actually do reduce the rate!

Coconut Encrusted Credit Reports
"Analyzing Your Credit Report"

> Make this recipe at least once a year. Changes to your credit history need to be reviewed consistently in order to prevent any surprises when applying for financing!

There was a time when your credit score was insignificant. Today, your take home pay takes a back seat to your credit score when bankers make lending decisions . How can you find out what your score is? In the old days, you needed an act of congress to get your hands on your credit report. Now, receiving copies of your credit report is easy.

Coconut Encrusted Credit Reports
"Analyzing Your Credit Report"

Ingredients

Credit Card Agencies – Equifax, Experian, TransUnion

Free annual, additional reports $9 fee for each

Your social security number

Internet access or telephone

Preparation

1. Order a copy of your credit report from each of the three major national credit bureaus: Equifax, Experian, and Trans Union. Telephone numbers and website addresses for the three agencies as follows:

Equifax	800-685-1111	website: www.equifax.com
Trans Union	800-690-1909	website: www.transunion.com
Experian	800-682-7654	website: www.experian.com

2. Once you receive your credit report, you should check the following information for accuracy: Your name, Your Date of Birth, Your Social Security Number, Your Addresses, Your Employment History

3. Review your debt. Check account numbers, outstanding balances, past due or late payment status, credit limits, and account status.

4. Make sure all accounts that you have closed are reflected on your credit report as closed.

5. Report any errors in writing to each of the credit agencies.

Recipe's Financial Nutritional Value
10=Degree of Risk
10=Long Tem Value or Growth Potential
10=Income Producing
0 =Tax Savings

Sample Portion of Credit Report

Sample Credit Report   Page 1 of 4

What's Your Credit Score Credit Report Company

Credit Report Prepared by What's Your Credit Score Credit Report Company for :

The Financial Chef
123 Main Str. Hometown USA
99999

Index:
- Potentially negative items
- Accounts in good standing
- Requests for your credit history
- Personal information
- Important message from Experian
- Contact us

Potentially Negative Items

Public Records

Credit grantors may carefully review the items listed below when they check your credit history. Please note that the account information connected with some public records, such as bankruptcy, also may appear with your credit items listed later in this report.

MAIN COUNTY CLERK

Address:	Identification Number:	Plaintiff:
123 MAINTOWN S	1	ANY COMMISSIONER O.
BUFFALO , NY 10000		

Status:	Status Details:
Civil claim paid.	This item was verified and updated on 06-2001

Date Filed:	Claim Amount:
10/15/2000	$200
Date Resolved:	Liability
01/04/2001	Amount:
	NA
Responsibility:	
INDIVIDUAL	

> This is bad stuff! Liens, Judgements and Bankruptcies are displayed here. Items under this section result usually from a court proceeding. Your credit score will suffer until these items are removed.

Credit Items

For your protection, the last few digits of your account numbers do not display.

ABCD BANKS

Address:	Account Number:
100 CENTER RD	1000000....
BUFFALO, NY 10000	
(555) 555-5555	

Status: Paid/Past due 60 days.

Date Opened:	Type:	Credit Limit/Original Amount:
10/1997	Installment	$523
Reported Since:	Terms:	High Balance:
11/1997	12 Months	NA
Date of Status:	Monthly	Recent Balance:
01/1999	Payment	$0 as of 01/1999
	$0	Recent Payment:
Last Reported:	Responsibility:	$0
01/1999	Individual	

> Even though the balance is zero, the account history will still show those times when payments were made late.

Account History:
60 days as of 12-1998
30 days as of 11-1998

Sample Credit Report

MAIN COLL AGENCIES

Address:	Account Number:	Original Creditor:
PO BOX 123	0123456789	TELEVISE CABLE COMM.
ANYTOWN, PA 10000		
(555) 555-5555		

Status: Collection account. $95 past due as of 4-2000.

Date Opened:	Type:		Credit Limit/Original Amount:
01/2000	Installment		$95
Reported Since:	Terms:		High Balance:
04/2000	NA		NA
Date of Status:	Monthly		Recent Balance:
04/2000	Payment:		$95 as of 04/2000
	$0		Recent Payment:
Last Reported:	Responsibility:		$0
04/2000	Individual		

Your statement: ITEM DISPUTED BY CONSUMER

Account History:
Collection as of 4-2000

> This item is being disputed by the Financial Chef. He try to resolve the issue so the item doesn't show on his credit report.

Accounts in Good Standing

back to top

AUTOMOBILE AUTO FINANCE

Address:	Account Number:
100 MAIN ST E	12345678998...
SMALLTOWN, MD 90001	
(555) 555-5555	

Status: Open/Never late.

Date Opened:	Type:	Credit Limit/Original Amount:
01/2000	Installment	$10,355
Reported Since:	Terms:	High Balance:
01/2000	65 Months	NA
Date of Status:	Monthly	Recent Balance:
08/2001	Payment:	$7,984 as of 08/2001
	$210	Recent Payment:
Last Reported:	Responsibility:	$0
08/2001	Individual	

MAIN

Address:	Account Number:
PO BOX 1234	1234567899876
FORT LAUDERDALE, FL 10009	

Status: Closed/Never late.

Date Opened:	Type:	Credit Limit/Original Amount:
03/1991	Revolving	NA
Reported Since:	Terms:	High Balance:
03/1991	1 Months	$3,228
Date of Status:	Monthly	Recent Balance:
08/2000	Payment:	$0 /paid as of 08/2000
	$0	Recent Payment:
Last Reported:	Responsibility:	$0
08/2000	Individual	

Your statement:
Account closed at consumer's request

Sample Credit Report   Page 3 of 4

Requests for Your Credit History   back to top

Requests Viewed By Others

We make your credit history available to your current and prospective creditors and employers as allowed by law. Personal data about you may be made available to companies whose products and services may interest you.

The section below lists all who have requested in the recent past to review your credit history as a result of actions involving you, such as the completion of a credit application or the transfer of an account to a collection agency, mortgage or loan application, etc. Creditors may view these requests when evaluating your creditworthiness.

HOMESALE REALTY CO
Address: Date of Request:
2000 S MAINROAD BLVD STE   07/16/2001
ANYTOWN CA 11111
(555) 555-5555
Comments:
Real estate loan on behalf of 1000 COPRORATE COMPANY. This inquiry is scheduled to continue on record until 8-2003.

ABC BANK
Address: Date of Request:
PO BOX 100   02/23/2001
BUFFALO NY 10000
(555) 555-5555
Comments:
Permissible purpose. This inquiry is scheduled to continue on record until 3-2003.

ANYTOWN FUNDING INC
Address: Date of Request:
100 W MAIN AVE STE 100   07/25/2000
INTOWN CA 10000
(555) 555-5555
Comments:
Permissible purpose. This inquiry is scheduled to continue on record until 8-2002.

Requests Viewed Only By You

The section below lists all who have a permissible purpose by law and have requested in the recent past to review your information. You may not have initiated these requests, so you may not recognize each source. We offer information about you to those with a permissible purpose, for example, to:

- other creditors who want to offer you preapproved credit;
- an employer who wishes to extend an offer of employment;
- a potential investor in assessing the risk of a current obligation;
- Experian or other credit reporting agencies to process a report for you;
- your existing creditors to monitor your credit activity (date listed may reflect only the most recent request).

We report these requests **only to you** as a record of activities. We **do not** provide this information to other creditors who evaluate your creditworthiness.

MAIN BANK USA
Address: Date of Request:
1 MAIN CTR AA 11   08/10/2001
BUFFALO NY 10000

MAINTOWN BANK
Address: Date of Request:
PO BOX 100   08/05/2001
MAINTOWNS DE 10000
(555) 555-5555

ANYTOWN DATA CORPS
Address: Date of Request:
2000 S MAINTOWN BLVD STE   07/16/2001
INTOWN CO 11111
(555) 555-5555

> Your credit score is hurt each time a company asks for your credit report. It looks like you're looking for more debt!

Personal Information

The following information is reported to us by you, your creditors and other sources. Each source may report your personal information differently, which may result in variations of your name, address, Social Security number, etc. As part of our fraud-prevention program, a notice with additional information may appear. As a security precaution, the Social Security number that you used to obtain this report is not displayed. The Geographical Code shown with each address identifies the state, county, census tract, block group and Metropolitan Statistical Area associated with each address.

Names:
The Financial Chef

Address: 123 Main Street
          Hometown, USA 99999
Type of Residence: Single Family
Geographical Code:0-176510-33-8840

Social Security number variations:

XXX-XX-XXXX

1971

Employers:
Cook Your Assets

Telephone numbers:
(555) 555 5555 Residential

Your Personal Statement

No general personal statements appear on your report.

Important Message From What's Your Credit Score Credit Report Company

By law, we cannot disclose certain medical information (relating to physical, mental, or behavioral health or condition). Although we do not generally collect such information, it could appear in the name of a data furnisher (i.e., "Cancer Center") that reports your payment history to us. If so, those names display in your report, but in reports to others they display only as MEDICAL PAYMENT DATA. Consumer statements included on your report at your request that contain medical information are disclosed to others.

Contacting Us

back to top

Contact address and phone number for your area will display here.

Still not clear what all those numbers mean? Read on...

Once you receive your credit report, you should check the following information for accuracy:

- Your name
- Your date of birth
- Your Social Security number
- Your addresses
- Your employment history

That was the easy part. You must also review your debt. Most debt can be separated into the following categories :

- Mortgage debt (your home or rental property financing)
- Revolving credit (your Visa, Discover, Mastercard etc)
- Installment Debt (your car, boat, rv or that way too expensive diamond tennis bracelet)
- Other (your American Express card or medical debt)

Displayed for the debt classifications is information including the account number, outstanding balance, past due or late payment status, account status, credit limit (if applicable) and any comments on the account. Verify that all information is reported accurately.

An error that may appear to be insignificant to you may have a substantial impact on your borrowing capabilities. For example, your Neiman Marcus Platinum Visa card is listed as having available credit of $ 25,000.00 rather than $ 5,000.00. Your borrowing potential will be computed as if you had used up your entire Neiman Marcus credit line.

Also, make certain all accounts that you have closed are no longer reflected on your report. Any bankruptcies should be taken off your report after 10 years. Tax liens, suits, and judgments should be dropped from your report seven years from their settlement date. Also, don't think that when seven years have passed, the credit reporting agency is just so efficient and will remember to remove the item.

Good luck with that one. Most likely you'll have to follow up with several phone calls to have the mark removed.

Also, any errors, that you discover, should be reported in writing to each of the credit agencies.

So what's a good credit score?
Grade your credit score using the table below.

720 and up AA
700 to 719 A
680 to 699 A-/B+
660 to 679 B+/B
640 to 659 B
620 to 639 B-/C+/C
600 to 619 C/D
580 to 599 D/F
579 and below F

The better your grade, the better interest rate you will be offered for financing. You may be thinking, "What's all the hype about? What makes this number so important?" Your credit score, also called a FICO score, is a major determinant of your financial health.

A sick score tends to spread and infect other areas of your financial life as well as your daily life. Have you ever experienced that long pregnant pause, while standing at a check out counter, waiting for a credit card charge to be approved? Worse than that tight feeling in your stomach while you pray for authorization is the feeling of total humiliation when your purchase is declined. I'm sure that many of us have heard those biting words "I'm sorry but there seems to be, well, lets say a problem, with your card. Do you have another way to pay?"

A healthy score helps keeps both your financial and daily life feeling fit. "What?" you think. "How can my score be so low!?"

Have you ever thought like this? Or do any of these situations apply to you?

- All I need to do is make the minimum payment; I don't have to pay-off the entire balance.

- I really need this, and the charge won't show until next month's statement.

- Wow, my credit card company just increased my credit limit. Now, I can replace that old TV I've been watching.

- If I open this new Macy's charge card, I can save 10% on this purchase! If I open this new Nordstrom's charge card, I can save 10% on this purchase. If I open...

If you haven't done any of these don't start now! They will only increase your debt problems!

Except for the obvious reason of not paying your bills when they come due, what are other causes for your credit score to be low?

- Length of revolving credit history is short
- Too many credit inquiries in the past 12 months
- Too many revolving and/or installment accounts
- Percentage of balances to credit limits is too high on revolving credit
- Number of accounts with delinquencies
- Unfavorable judgments or collections

How can you raise your score?

Let's ask the financial chef to answer this question. The financial chef advises you to:

- Pay your creditors on time each month.
- Don't max your credit card limits. Try to keep your available credit at least 25% of your card's limit. Also, try to limit the number of credit cards you own.
- Try to keep your oldest credit cards active. If you want to close an account, cancel your most recently acquired credit cards.
- Keep credit inquiries to a minimum. Excessive credit inquiries are interpreted to be a sign that you are actively seeking additional credit.
- Not charge that new pair of Jimmy Choo shoes or that ultra-soft Dolce cashmere sweater – SORRY LADIES!

You will want to make this recipe once a year. Changes to your credit history need to be reviewed consistently in order to prevent any surprises when applying for financing.

Congratulations, you've cooked another asset!

Here's a financial diet tip!

Pay your bills on time! Better yet, pay your bills early!

Okay, I'll admit to having completely forgotten to pay a credit card bill. You too? Did you pay the late fee? Don't do it! Always ask if the charges can be reversed. The worst they can say is "No". If they agree, then you have $39.00 to spend towards a new outfit! What? Did I say outfit? I meant you have $39.00 to put into your savings account!

Financial Chef

Bistro Bruschetta Budgets
"Adopting a Budget"

A budget can fail because it's not initially funded with enough money. Starbuck's keep a " bank" in their cash register drawer to start the day's sales activity. Each day your budget should start with a "bank" too. At the end of the day, you should still have your "bank" to start the next day

Most people think budget is a four letter word but it's not. The budget blues come from setting unrealistic goals.

You should be able to embrace your budget, make it yours. This is why the word, adopt, is used to describe the budget process. Webster's Dictionary defines adopt as to take up and use one's own. Your budget is yours and only yours. You will be the one who has to adhere to it. You want to make sure you can live by the budget you have created.

Bistro Bruschetta Budgets
"Adopting a Budget"

Ingredients

List of your income

List of your expenses

Personal budget computer software or

Personal budget workbook found in most office supply stores

Realistic goals & willpower

Preparation

1. *Purchase either budget computer software or a personal budget workbook found in most office supply stores.*

2. List all your sources of income– net paycheck amount, dividends, interest, part time income, alimony, child support, pensions, social security .

3. *List all fixed expenses- those bills that have the same payment month to month.*

4. *List all variable expenses—those expenditures whose amounts change from month to month.*

    Usually, variable expenses will increase or decrease based upon your usage or consumption and price changes.

5. *Subtract both the fixed and variable expenses from the sources of income amount. If there is any $$ leftover ... well... YIPEE!*

Recipe's Financial Nutritional Value
20=Degree of Risk
30=Long Tem Value or Growth Potential
20=Income Producing
10 =Tax Savings

Portion of Sample Budget

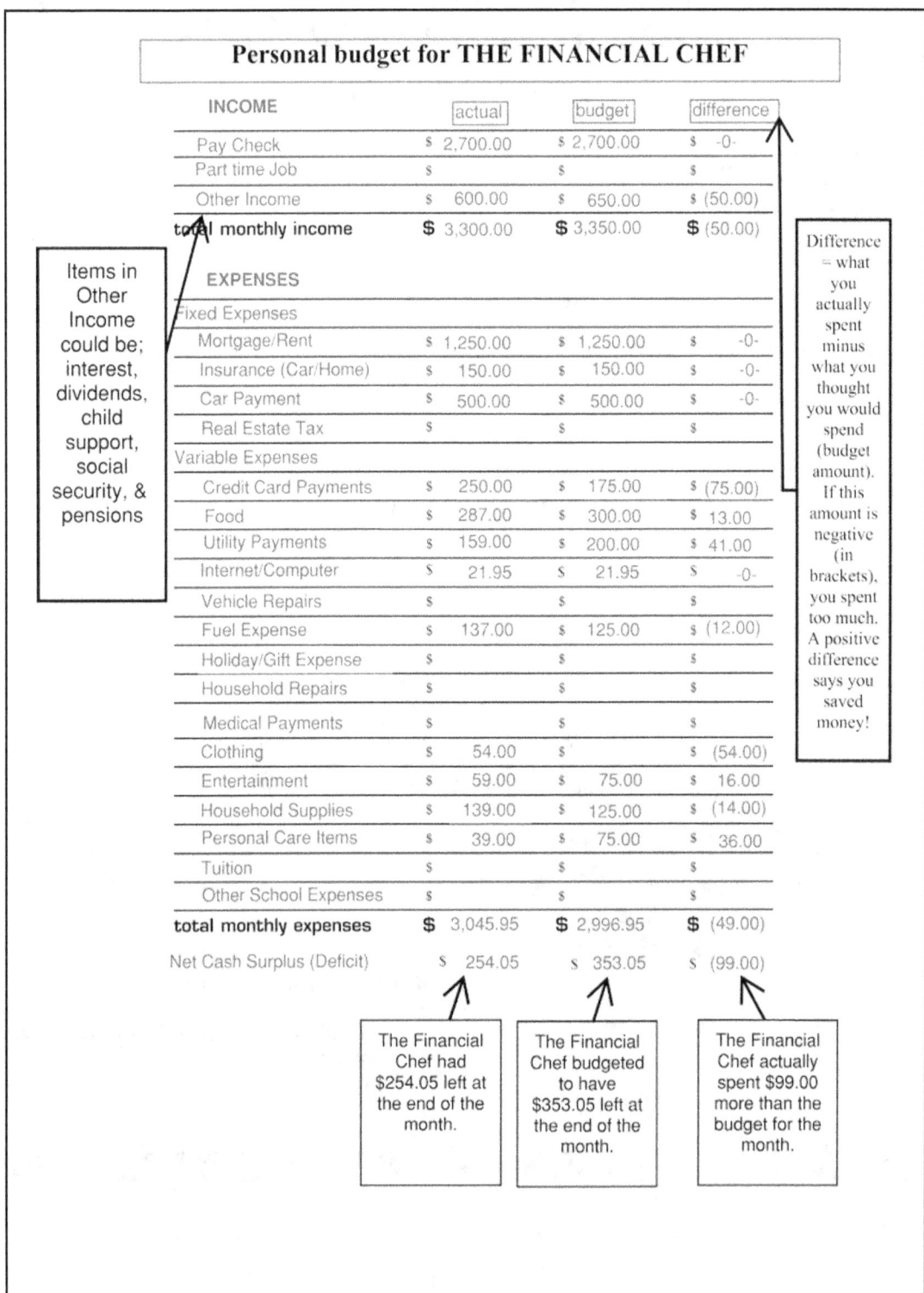

Personal budget for THE FINANCIAL CHEF

INCOME	actual	budget	difference
Pay Check	$ 2,700.00	$ 2,700.00	$ -0-
Part time Job	$	$	$
Other Income	$ 600.00	$ 650.00	$ (50.00)
total monthly income	$ 3,300.00	$ 3,350.00	$ (50.00)
EXPENSES			
Fixed Expenses			
Mortgage/Rent	$ 1,250.00	$ 1,250.00	$ -0-
Insurance (Car/Home)	$ 150.00	$ 150.00	$ -0-
Car Payment	$ 500.00	$ 500.00	$ -0-
Real Estate Tax	$	$	$
Variable Expenses			
Credit Card Payments	$ 250.00	$ 175.00	$ (75.00)
Food	$ 287.00	$ 300.00	$ 13.00
Utility Payments	$ 159.00	$ 200.00	$ 41.00
Internet/Computer	$ 21.95	$ 21.95	$ -0-
Vehicle Repairs	$	$	$
Fuel Expense	$ 137.00	$ 125.00	$ (12.00)
Holiday/Gift Expense	$	$	$
Household Repairs	$	$	$
Medical Payments	$	$	$
Clothing	$ 54.00	$	$ (54.00)
Entertainment	$ 59.00	$ 75.00	$ 16.00
Household Supplies	$ 139.00	$ 125.00	$ (14.00)
Personal Care Items	$ 39.00	$ 75.00	$ 36.00
Tuition	$	$	$
Other School Expenses	$	$	$
total monthly expenses	$ 3,045.95	$ 2,996.95	$ (49.00)
Net Cash Surplus (Deficit)	$ 254.05	$ 353.05	$ (99.00)

Items in Other Income could be; interest, dividends, child support, social security, & pensions

Difference = what you actually spent minus what you thought you would spend (budget amount). If this amount is negative (in brackets), you spent too much. A positive difference says you saved money!

The Financial Chef had $254.05 left at the end of the month.

The Financial Chef budgeted to have $353.05 left at the end of the month.

The Financial Chef actually spent $99.00 more than the budget for the month.

Need more help creating a budget? Read on...

Most people think budget is a four- letter word but it's not. It's six! Sorry, that was a bad one...

The budget blues come from setting unrealistic goals. Take Debtor Debbie; she wants to buy a new plasma TV. Her credit cards are already screaming past their limits. Her only choice is to adopt a budget that will allow her to set aside enough money to make her big purchase.

She allows herself $100.00 a month for grocery purchases. Already she's failed.

Why? Well, Debtor Debbie is a gourmet cook and loves to splurge on her boyfriend by creating him extravagant meals. It's only the 10th of the month and she's already surpassed her budget, buying black truffle infused olive oil at $ 10 an ounce and filet mignon steaks at $ 26.99 per pound. He's happy, she's not. She wants to watch Rachel Ray's 30 minute meals on a new plasma TV.

Unfortunately, she has set herself up for failure by only allowing herself $100.00 a month for grocery purchases. Defeated, Debtor Debbie ditches the budget. At the end of the month, she has $5 remaining in her checking account.

LESSON TO BE LEARNED – Budgets have to be set with REALISTIC goals that can reasonably be met.

Perhaps Debtor Debbie could have cut back some where else. Maybe, she could have gone without purchasing any new clothes for the month.

You should be able to embrace your budget, make it yours. This is why the word, adopt, is used to describe the budget process. Webster's Dictionary defines adopt as to take up and use one's own. Your budget is yours and only yours. You will be the one who has to adhere to it. You want to make sure you can live by the budget you have created.

Why even budget at all? One good reason to budget is to prevent pre-paycheck panic. All of us have suffered pre-paycheck panic. Debtor Debbie raids her stash of spare change to buy an Egg McMuffin for breakfast. Is this a problem? Yes, especially since she raids on a Monday and her payday isn't until Friday. Does this situation sound vaguely familiar? For many of us, this is an on-going ritual.

The feelings of frustration and defeat that accompany this scenario should make you want to change your spending habits. Perhaps you're ready for a financial facelift by adopting a budget.

Important events in your life that can spark the need for a budget are:

- Wedding
- Divorce
- Having a child
- New job
- Saving for a big purchase
- Moving/Buying a house

Understanding what is controllable and what is not is key to developing a manageable budget. Controllable items are predictable and consistent in nature or "fixed." Uncontrollable items are unpredictable and fluctuating in nature or "variable."

In order to create a budget, you must account for both your income and expenses. Generally, income is easier to budget for than are expenses. Let's prepare a budget by deciding the simplest ingredients (income) first and then adding more difficult ingredients (expenses) next to complete our recipe.

The most obvious source of income is your paycheck. Use net pay not your gross pay for budgeting. If you're a salaried employee, this amount is generally fixed. Don't forget to include ancillary reimbursements you receive in addition to your regular wages. Some of these extras might include auto allowance, travel and entertainment reimbursements, and medical reimbursements.

If you work on commission or are an hourly employee, forecasting your income may become more difficult because you don't know how much you'll end up receiving. Better to underestimate your income leaving a surplus than overestimate leaving a deficit.

If you're self-employed, use net earnings to calculate your income. Net earnings are the amount of income remaining after you have deducted all your business expenses and anticipated income taxes.

Other income sources that can be added to your budget are interest income, dividend income, part-time jobs, alimony, child support, pensions, and social security.

Expenses may be broken down into fixed and variable categories. Forecasting fixed expenses is straightforward. Variable expenses are more difficult to estimate.

Fixed Expenses
- ✓ Rent or mortgage (including principal, tax, insurance)
- ✓ Vehicle payments
- ✓ Medical or heath insurance(suggested caps)
- ✓ Garbage/Trash Removal
- ✓ Cable or Satellite TV bills
- ✓ Disability Insurance
- ✓ Other Loan Payments (ie: Second Mortgage)
- ✓ Student Loans
- ✓ Child Support Payments
- ✓ Alimony Payments
- ✓ Computer/Internet Access

Variable Expenses
- ✓ Utilities – (phone, electric, gas and water)
- ✓ Food Costs
- ✓ Credit Card Payments
- ✓ Fuel and Other Auto Expenses
- ✓ Clothing, Laundry, DryCleaning
- ✓ Child Care/Babysitter
- ✓ Pet/Veterinary Costs
- ✓ Entertainment (movies, dining out, sports)
- ✓ Holidays, Church, Charities

Also, tricky to predict, is the extraordinary expense An example of an extraordinary expense would be braces for your daughter's teeth to cure her overbite.

Extraordinary expenses would also include replacement of household appliances and fixtures that have broken or given out. An extraordinary expense usually is unexpected thus making it difficult to provide for when budgeting A reserve fund can be started to accumulate monies to pay for potential extraordinary items. The dollars set aside in the reserve fund become a fixed expense of your budget.

Not starting with enough initial funds or money is one reason a budget can fail. Retail stores keep a money bank in their cash register drawer. This is necessary to start the day's sales activity. The same holds true for your budget.

Let's say your auto insurance annual paymentis due in January. If you budget the entire payment in January, you probably won't have enough cash to pay your other expenses for the month. You need to use your cash bank as a temporary funding source. If you budget the auto insurance over the entire year, by the end of the year, you will have "repaid" the funds from the cash bank.

You're probably thinking, "How do I keep track of all this? It all seems pretty complicated." Investing in a computer software program for your personal budget is a smart move.

Software programs are easy to use and only cost about $50.00. Not only can you save time paying a majority of your bills on-line, personal budgeting software lets you know if you are still within your budget at any time. The programs also show you the specific areas that are over or under budget. Most importantly, the budget software does all the work for you.

You've adopted a budget and are trying to live by it. However, when the end of the month comes, you can't understand where all the money has gone.

Let's ask the financial chef why this happens.

It's the little things that add up. Review the fact finder worksheet on the next page and you'll discover how little expenses can make a big difference.

WHERE DOES IT ALL GO? FACT FINDER

Expense	Per Unit Cost	Annual Cost	Cost After 20 Years
• Daily Starbuck's Coffee	$4	$1,460	$29,200
• Weekly desert when dining out	$4	$208	$4,160
• Soda instead of water with lunch	$1.75	$638.75	$12,775
• Smoking a pack of cigarettes a day	$4	$1,460	$29,200
• Not having a free checking account	$12	$ 144	$2,880
• Pay 10 bills on-line monthly instead of by mail	$.37	$44.40	$888
• One manicure per month	$24	$288	$5,760
• Purchase one magazine per month	$5	$60	$1,200
Total Annual Expenses		**$4,303.15**	**$86,063**

You can see from the above, how quickly your money can be spent.

Here's a more startling realization. Lets say you earn $ 15/hour. You would have to work 7 weeks straight each year just to pay for cigarettes, manicures, coffee and an occasional magazine!

Make your own spreadsheet from this worksheet by eliminating from your spending habits unnecessary items. You'll be surprised how little a sacrifice this change will be. Just don't pick up new bad spending habits to replace the old ones.

Finally, don't be afraid to go over budget. Yes, I did say that. Sometimes, an opportunity may come along that is just too good to pass up. Let's say you spot a beautiful couch at Conran's, marked down from $ 3,500 to just $599. You think it must be mismarked, but the salesman assures you the price is right. The couch has a palm tree pattern that will match perfectly your palm tree décor. Your existing couch is showing its age with a myriad of food mishaps from late night movie watching. You think, " But a new couch is not in my budget." I say, "Go for it!" You'll have to replace the couch soon anyway, and where are you going to find one for that price and with those cute little palm trees? You could almost think of the couch as an investment. A budget is meant to be flexible. Perhaps you can cut back and do your nails yourself for a few months and sell some old clothes to a consignment shop.

Congratulations, you've cooked another asset!

Here's a financial diet tip!

Don't get upside down on your auto purchase. You're upside down if your auto loan is more than what you can expect to get by selling your car. You can't pay off the loan with the money from the sale, so you're either stuck with the car and the payments or you have to come up with more money to get out. Shorter loan periods (ie: 3yrs) help to avoid this dilemma.

Bacon Wrapped W-4 Forms

"Filling in a W-4 Form"

Careful, if you falsely claim too many withholdings you could be hit with a $500.00 penalty!

What is a W-4 Form? Many people view the W-4 Form as just another government form used to take money out of their paycheck to pay for income taxes. Basically, this is true. Careful though, if you don't fill the form out correctly you may owe loads of taxes at the end of the year.

Bacon Wrapped W-4 Forms
"Filling in a W-4 Form"

Ingredients

A job! (employer)

IRS Form W-4

Social security number

Last resort—IRS Publication 919– helpful resource tool
that can be downloaded from IRS website (www.irs.gov)

Preparation

1. Start easy– fill in your name, address and social security number.

2. Determine if you are single, married or married withholding at a single rate. First two are pretty easy to figure but what about married withholding at single rate? You may want to check this box if you're married and both you and your spouse are both working.

3. Calculate the number of allowances you will report. Basically (see the chart in the W-4 recipe pages that follow for additional details).

You	= 1 exemption
Your Spouse	= 1 exemption
Your Dependents	= 1 exemption for each dependent
Fluffy—your dog	= no exemption—sorry!

4. If you think you still need to have more money withheld from your paycheck, put an amount in Line 6 and that amount with be withheld from each paycheck.

5. Sign the form at the bottom and keep a copy for yourself.

Recipe's Financial Nutritional Value
10=Degree of Risk
10=Long Tem Value or Growth Potential
10=Income Producing
0 =Tax Savings

Sample W-4 Form

> Fill out this W-4? I don't like this job already--- there's too much paperwork...

Purpose. Complete Form W-4 so that your employer can withhold the correct federal income tax from your pay. Because your tax situation may change, you may want to refigure your withholding each year.

Exemption from withholding. If you are exempt, complete **only** lines 1, 2, 3, 4, and 7 and sign the form to validate it. Your exemption for 2007 expires February 16, 2008. See Pub. 505, Tax Withholding and Estimated Tax.

Note. You cannot claim exemption from withholding if (a) your income exceeds $850 and includes more than $300 of unearned income (for example, interest and dividends) and (b) another person can claim you as a dependent on their tax return.

Basic instructions. If you are not exempt, complete the **Personal Allowances Worksheet** below. The worksheets on page 2 adjust your withholding allowances based on

adjustments to income, or two-earner/multiple job situations. Complete all worksheets that apply. However, you may claim fewer (or zero) allowances.

Head of household. Generally, you may claim head of household filing status on your tax return only if you are unmarried and pay more than 50% of the costs of keeping up a home for yourself and your dependent(s) or other qualifying individuals.

Tax credits. You can take projected tax credits into account in figuring your allowable number of withholding allowances. Credits for child or dependent care expenses and the child tax credit may be claimed using the **Personal Allowances Worksheet** below. See Pub. 919, How Do I Adjust My Tax Withholding, for information on converting your other credits into withholding allowances.

Nonwage income. If you have a large amount of nonwage income, such as interest or dividends, consider making estimated tax payments using Form 1040-ES, Estimated Tax

additional tax. If you have pension or annuity income, see Pub. 919 to find out if you should adjust your withholding on Form W-4 or W-4P.

Two earners/Multiple jobs. If you have a working spouse or more than one job, figure the total number of allowances you are entitled to claim on all jobs using worksheets from only one Form W-4. Your withholding usually will be most accurate when all allowances are claimed on the Form W-4 for the highest paying job and zero allowances are claimed on

exceed $130,000 (Single) or $180,000 (Married).

> Is "Little Joey" part of an after school program that you pay for? Does it cost you at least $1,500? Enter a "1" for an additional allowance.

Personal Allowances Worksheet (Keep for your records.)

A Enter "1" for **yourself** if no one else can claim you as a dependent . . . . **A**

B Enter "1" if: { • You are single and have only one job; or
                     • You are married, have only one job, and your spouse does not work; or } . . **B**
                     • Your wages from a second job or your spouse's wages (or the total of both) are $1,000 or less.

C Enter "1" for your **spouse**. But, you may choose to enter "-0-" if you are married and have either a working spouse or more than one job. (Entering "-0-" may help you avoid having too little tax withheld.) . . . . . . **C**

D Enter number of **dependents** (other than your spouse or yourself) you will claim on your tax return . . . . **D**

E Enter "1" if you will file as **head of household** on your tax return (see conditions under **Head of household** above) **E**

F Enter "1" if you have at least $1,500 of **child or dependent care expenses** for which you plan to claim a credit **F**
   (**Note.** Do **not** include child support payments. See Pub. 503, Child and Dependent Care Expenses, for details.)

G **Child Tax Credit** (including additional child tax credit). See Pub 972, Child Tax Credit, for more information.
   • If your total income will be less than $57,000 ($85,000 if married), enter "2" for each eligible child.
   • If your total income will be between $57,000 and $84,000 ($85,000 and $119,000 if married), enter "1" for each eligible child plus "1" **additional** if you have 4 or more eligible children. . . . . **G**

H Add lines A through G and enter total here. (**Note.** This may be different from the number of exemptions you claim on your tax return.) ▶ **H**

For accuracy, complete all worksheets that apply.
   • If you plan to **itemize or claim adjustments to income** and want to reduce your withholding, see the **Deductions and Adjustments Worksheet** on page 2.
   • If you have **more than one job or are married and you and your spouse both work** and the combined earnings from all jobs exceed $40,000 ($25,000 if married) see the **Two-Earners/Multiple Jobs Worksheet** on page 2 to avoid having too little tax withheld.
   • If **neither of the above situations applies, stop here** and enter the number from line H on line 5 of Form W-4 below.

- - - - - - - - - - Cut here and give Form W-4 to your employer. Keep the top part for your records. - - - - - - - - - -

Form W-4
Department of the Treasury
Internal Revenue Service

Employee's Withholding Allowance Certificate

▶ Whether you are entitled to claim a certain number of allowances or exemption from withholding is subject to review by the IRS. Your employer may be required to send a copy of this form to the IRS.

OMB No. 1545-0074

2007

1 Type or print your first name and middle initial.   Last name   Your social security number

   Home address (number and street or rural route)

   City or town, state, and ZIP code

3 ☐ Single ☐ Married ☐ Married, but withhold at higher Single rate.
   Note. If married, but legally separated, or spouse is a nonresident alien, check the "Single" box.

4 If your last name differs from that shown on your social security card, check here. You must call 1-800-772-1213 for a replacement card. ▶ ☐

> Place the amount from "H" to Line Item #5

5 Total number of allowances you are claiming (from line H above **or** from the applicable worksheet on page 2) **5**

6 Additional amount, if any, you want withheld from each paycheck . . . . **6** $

7 I claim exemption from withholding for 2007, and I certify that I meet **both** of the following conditions for exemption.
   • Last year I had a right to a refund of **all** federal income tax withheld because I had **no** tax liability **and**
   • This year I expect a refund of **all** federal income tax withheld because I expect to have **no** tax liability.
   If you meet both conditions, write "Exempt" here ▶ **7**

> You may want your employer to withhold additional federal tax if you have considerable sources of other income; ie: interest, dividends, alimony received, capital gains etc.

Under penalties of perjury, I declare that I have examined this certificate and to the best of my knowledge and belief, it is true, correct, and complete.

Employee's signature (Form is not valid unless you sign it.) ▶

8 Employer's name and address (Employer: Complete lines 8 and 10 only if sending to the IRS.)

9 Office code (optional)

10 Employer identification number (EIN)

For Privacy Act and Paperwork Reduction Act Notice, see page 2.   Cat. No. 10220Q   Form **W-4** (2007)

Form W-4 (2007) Page **2**

Deductions and Adjustments Worksheet

Note. Use this worksheet *only* if you plan to itemize deductions, claim certain credits, or claim adjustments to income on your 2007 tax return.

1. Enter an estimate of your 2007 itemized deductions. These include qualifying home mortgage interest, charitable contributions, state and local taxes, medical expenses in excess of 7.5% of your income, and [...] uce your itemized deductions if your income [...] Worksheet 2 in Pub. 919 for details.) ... **1** $ _____

> Review this section if you itemize your deductions on your personal tax return.

($ 5,350 if single or married filing separately ...   **2** $ _____

3. **Subtract** line 2 from line 1. If zero or less, enter "-0-" ... **3** $ _____
4. Enter an estimate of your 2007 adjustments to income, including alimony, deductible IRA contributions, and student loan interest **4** $ _____
5. **Add** lines 3 and 4 and enter the total. (Include any amount for credits from *Worksheet 8* in Pub. 919) ... **5** $ _____
6. Enter an estimate of your 2007 nonwage income (such as dividends or interest) ... **6** $ _____
7. **Subtract** line 6 from line 5. If zero or less, enter "-0-" ... **7** $ _____
8. **Divide** the amount on line 7 by $3,400 and enter the result here. Drop any fraction ... **8** _____
9. Enter the number from the **Personal Allowances Worksheet**, line H, page 1 ... **9** _____
10. **Add** lines 8 and 9 and enter the total here. If you plan to use the **Two-Earners/Multiple Jobs Worksheet**, also enter this total on line 1 below. Otherwise, **stop here** and enter this total on Form W-4, line 5, page 1 **10** _____

Two-Earners/Multiple Jobs Worksheet (See *Two earners/multiple jobs* on page 1.)

Note. Use this worksheet *only* if the instructions under line H on page 1 direct you here.

1. Enter the number from line H, page 1 (or from line 10 above if you used the **Deductions and Adjustments Worksheet** **1** _____

> Review this section if you or you & your spouse have multiple jobs.

[...]g job and enter it here. **However,** if [...]e $50,000 or less, do not enter more ... **2** _____

3. If line 1 **is more than or equal to** line 2, subtract line 2 from line 1. Enter the result here (if zero, enter "-0-") and on Form W-4, line 5, page 1. **Do not** use the rest of this worksheet ... **3** _____

Note. If line 1 is *less than* line 2, enter "-0-" on Form W-4, line 5, page 1. Complete lines 4-9 below to calculate the additional withholding amount necessary to avoid a year-end tax bill.

4. Enter the number from line 2 of this worksheet ... **4** _____
5. Enter the number from line 1 of this worksheet ... **5** _____
6. Subtract line 5 from line 4 ... **6** _____
7. Find the amount in **Table 2** below that applies to the **HIGHEST** paying job and enter it here ... **7** $ _____
8. **Multiply** line 7 by line 6 and enter the result here. This is the additional annual withholding needed ... **8** $ _____
9. Divide line 8 by the number of pay periods remaining in 2007. For example, divide by 26 if you are paid every two weeks and you complete this form in December 2006. Enter the result here and on Form W-4, line 6, page 1. This is the additional amount to be withheld from each paycheck ... **9** $ _____

Table 1

Married Filing Jointly		All Others	
If wages from LOWEST paying job are—	Enter on line 2 above	If wages from LOWEST paying job are—	Enter on line 2 above
$0 - $4,500	0	$0 - $6,000	0
4,501 - 9,000	1	6,001 - 12,000	1
9,001 - 18,000	2	12,001 - 19,000	2
18,001 - 22,000	3	19,001 - 26,000	3
22,001 - 26,000	4	26,001 - 35,000	4
26,001 - 32,000	5	35,001 - 50,000	5
32,001 - 38,000	6	50,001 - 65,000	6
38,001 - 46,000	7	65,001 - 80,000	7
46,001 - 55,000	8	80,001 - 90,000	8
55,001 - 60,000	9	90,001 - 120,000	9
60,001 - 65,000	10	120,001 and over	10
65,001 - 75,000	11		
75,001 - 95,000	12		
95,001 - 105,000	13		
105,001 - 120,000	14		
120,001 and over	15		

Table 2

Married Filing Jointly		All Others	
If wages from HIGHEST paying job are—	Enter on line 7 above	If wages from HIGHEST paying job are—	Enter on line 7 above
$0 - $65,000	$510	$0 - $35,000	$510
65,001 - 120,000	850	35,001 - 80,000	850
120,001 - 170,000	950	80,001 - 150,000	950
170,001 - 300,000	1,120	150,001 - 340,000	1,120
300,001 and over	1,190	340,001 and over	1,190

Still need more help filling out that pesky Form W-4? Read On...

For what is supposed to be a simple IRS Form, the W-4 causes millions of Americans confusion and stress. Often mistaken for its counterpart the W-2 Form, the W-4 is often misunderstood.

First, the greater the allowances you claim, the less your employer will withhold from your paycheck. Seems like a backwards way of thinking to me. You're also probably thinking, Great! I'll declare lots of allowances and I'll take home a bigger paycheck!" Not so fast, when it comes time to file your taxes, you'll be shocked into hysteria when you have to write the IRS a big fat check. Owe too much and you may even have to pay a penalty.

So what exactly is an allowance or withholding exemption? Technically, a withholding exemption releases a certain dollar amount of your earnings from tax withholding. Wow, that was busy. Okay, an exemption is the amount of your pay that isn't going to be taxed because you have some deductions. Better?

So how many allowances do you have? Let's start at ground zero.

Can you be declared a dependant of someone else? Essentially, is someone else still taking care of you? Usually, a child, who is a student, would be a dependant of someone else; his or her parents. Also, an elderly person, living with his or her children, would be a dependant of someone else. If this is the case, then you have zero allowances or exemptions.

Next, are you single? This earns you an additional allowance.

Are you married? This earns you another allowance. Who says being married doesn't have its benefits?

The next step focuses on the number of jobs. If you have more than one job If you have more than one job, make sure you claim zero allowances at your second job. Claiming "exempt" is NOT the same as claiming zero. By claiming zero, the highest amount of tax is withheld from your paycheck.

You are exempt from income tax withholding only if your income for the year will be less than a certain amount. This amount changes each year depending on inflation. If you are exempt, skip lines 5 and 6, and write "EXEMPT" on line 7 of Form W-4.

Confusing? Let's simplify. Generally speaking, the following chart summarizes increases and decreases in withholding allowances.

Event or Situation	Increase Allowances (Larger Paycheck)	Decrease Allowances (Smaller Paycheck)
Increases in Investment Income		yes
Child/Children	yes	
Two Jobs for one individual		yes
Both spouses working		yes
Parents qualify as dependents	yes	
Qualify for child tax credits	yes	
Qualify for child care expenses	yes	
Qualify to itemize your deductions	yes	

At the beginning of every year, your employer should provide you with a new Form W-4 to complete. This isn't the only time to review your withholding allowances. Review for events such as marriage, divorce, having a child, purchasing a home, receiving social security benefits while still employed, death of a working spouse or increases in income (ie: interest income) not subject to withholdings.

You may be thinking "Why bother? If I owe additional taxes, I'll just write Uncle Sam a check at the end of the year. Careful, if you falsely claim too many withholdings you could be hit with a $500.00 penalty!

Congratulations, you've cooked another asset!

Section IV

Entrees for the
Prime of Life

Picture this. Your significant other calls in the middle of your workday. He asks if you want him to make reservations for Saturday night at The Rustic Bistro. The Rustic Bistro is only the hottest new restaurant in town. You scream "Yes!" with delight.

Walking through the dining room illuminated by beautiful wood carved chandeliers you're led to your table. Large overstuffed booths constructed of Hawaiian Koa wood offer seclusion from the other patrons. The atmosphere has set the mood for an amazing dining experience. Imagine when the waiter hands you the menu you find that you only have one choice of entrée. Baked lobster tails stuffed with crab risotto is the item of the evening.

For many this entrée would be decadent; for you, allergic to shellfish, it's a disaster. This restaurant could make the best baked lobster tails in the world, but without any other entrée choices, many of their customers will be unhappy. This is why most restaurants have a variety of entrees. People have different needs. While chicken works for some diners, beef may work better for others.

The same principal holds true for the recipes of the Entrees for the Prime of Life section of this cookbook. Prime of Life entrée recipes should be used to optimize life-changing events. Purchasing a house, securing life insurance, and saving for your children's college education are just a few. People have many financial needs, with those needs varying from person to person. Saving for college may be critical to a family with five kids while a single female in her forties may find long term care insurance to be vital. Having options and then knowing how to choose from the options is crucial to successful financial health.

After reading the recipes in this section, you should have the groundwork to access your own financial needs. You'll have a basis to draw from and use to plan for life changing events instead of reacting to them.

House Purchase with Hollandaise

"Purchasing a Home"

> You may want to purchase a home for sale by owner and save money on those pesky realtor fees!

Whether you're interested in a small fixer upper or a million dollar plus home on the beach, purchasing a home can be intimidating. The number of decisions to make is staggering. Brick vs wood vs concrete block or one story vs two story or colonial vs contemporary or near schools vs near shopping. Ahhh... I envy the "old lady in the shoe" - how simple was that!

House Purchase with Hollandaise

"Purchasing a Home"

Ingredients

Real estate agent– especially first time buyers

Real estate attorney & title company– usually provided by the real estate agent

Your dream home

Purchase contract

Money / Deposit

Mortgage (unless you don't need one– which would make me very jealous)

Preparation

1. *Decide between renting and buying*
2. *Determine How much you can afford*
3. *Find a real estate agent (especially if this is your first home purchase). It is also advisable to retain a real estate tax attorney.*
4. *Start house hunting. When you find a house you like make sure you review the neighborhood too.*
5. *Make an offer and sign a purchase contract. At this time you will have to provide a deposit. Ask your attorney about contingencies. These are ways to get out of the contract.*
6. *Get professional inspections. Do a "walk through" -write down items you would like corrected before closing. If the house is for sale "as is" then this will not be an option for you.*
7. *Apply for the mortgage.*
8. *Do a "final walk through" to make sure that nothing has changed since your last inspection.*
9. *Go to the Closing. Basically a day to sign a lot of paperwork and get the keys to your new home. This can also be done through the mail if more convenient.*

Recipe's Financial Nutritional Value
30=Degree of Risk
60=Long Tem Value or Growth Potential
20=Income Producing
30=Tax Savings

Sample Closing Statement

OMB NO. 2502-0265

A

U.S. DEPARTMENT OF HOUSING & URBAN DEVELOPMENT

SETTLEMENT STATEMENT

B. TYPE OF LOAN:
1. ☐ FHA 2. ☐ FmHA 3. X CONV. UNINS. 4. ☐ VA 5. ☐ CONV. INS.
6. FILE NUMBER: SAMPLE
7. LOAN NUMBER:
8. MORTGAGE INS. CASE NUMBER:

C. NOTE: This form is furnished to give you a statement of actual settlement costs. Amounts paid to and by the settlement agent are shown. Items marked "[POC]" were paid outside the closing; they are shown here for informational purposes and are not included in the totals.

D. NAME AND ADDRESS OF BUYER:	E. NAME AND ADDRESS OF SELLER:	F. NAME AND ADDRESS OF LENDER:
The Financial Chef 123 Main Street Hometown, USA 99999	Debtor Debbie 123 Easy Street Hometown, USA 99999	ABC Lenders 123 Lender Street Hometown, USA 99999

G. PROPERTY LOCATION:	H. SETTLEMENT AGENT: ABC Title Company	I. SETTLEMENT DATE:
123 Easy Street Happytown, USA 11111	PLACE OF SETTLEMENT: ABC Title Company's office	2-01-08

Price you and seller agree to

J. SUMMARY OF BUYER'S TRANSACTION		K. SUMMARY OF SELLER'S TRANSACTION	
100. GROSS AMOUNT DUE FROM BUYER:		400. GROSS AMOUNT DUE TO SELLER:	
101. Contract Sales Price	200,000	401. Contract Sales Price	200,000
102. Personal Property		402. Personal Property	
103. Settlement Charges to Buyer (Line 1400)	1,950	403.	
104.		404.	
105.		405.	
Adjustments For Items Paid By Seller in advance		*Adjustments For Items Paid By Seller in advance*	
106. City/Town Taxes　　to		406. City/Town Taxes　　to	
107. County Taxes　　to		407. County Taxes　　to	
		408. Assessments	
		409.	
		410.	
		411.	
		412.	
120. GROSS AMOUNT DUE FROM BUYER	201,950	420. GROSS AMOUNT DUE TO SELLER	200,000
200. AMOUNTS PAID BY OR IN BEHALF OF BUYER:		500. REDUCTIONS IN AMOUNT DUE TO SELLER	
201. Deposit or earnest money	20,000	501.	
202. Principal Amount of New Loan(s)	150,000	502.	
203. Existing loan(s) taken subject to		503.	13,400
204.		504.	115,294
205.		505.	
206.		506.	
207.		507.	
208.		508.	
209.		509.	
Adjustments For Items Unpaid By Seller			
210. City/Town Taxes　　to		510. City/Town Taxes　　to	
211. County Taxes　1 mth　to	254	511. County Taxes　1 mth　to	254
212. Assessments　　to		512. Assessments　　to	
213.		513.	
214.		514.	
215.		515.	
216.		516.	
217.		517.	
218.		518.	
219.		519.	
220. TOTAL PAID BY/FOR BUYER	170,254	520. TOTAL REDUCTION AMOUNT DUE SELLER	128,948
300. CASH AT SETTLEMENT FROM/TO BUYER:		600. CASH AT SETTLEMENT TO/FROM SELLER:	
301. Gross Amount Due From Buyer (Line 120)		601. Gross Amount Due To Seller (Line 420)	
302. Less Amount Paid By/For Buyer (Line 220)	( )	602. Less Reductions Due Seller (Line 520)	( )
303. CASH (✓ FROM)(TO) BUYER	31,696　0-00	603. CASH (✓ TO)(FROM) SELLER	71,052　0-00

Down payment seller requests up front- to make sure you're a serious buyer

Closing costs charged - see detail on second page

Unless, buyers assumes your existing mortgage (very rare), you must pay off the balance of your mortgage at closing. The bank will provide you with the amount.

The undersigned hereby acknowledge receipt of a completed copy of pages 1&2 of this statement & any attachments referred to herein.

Buyer

Seller

Page 2

L. SETTLEMENT CHARGES

700. TOTAL COMMISSION Based on Price	$ 200,000 @ 6 %		PAID FROM BUYER'S FUNDS AT SETTLEMENT	PAID FROM SELLER'S FUNDS AT SETTLEMENT
Division of Commission (line 700) as Follows:				
701 $	to			
702 $	to			
703. Commission Paid at Settlement				
704	to			12,000

800. ITEMS PAYABLE IN CONNECTION WITH LOAN

801. Loan Origination Fee	%	to
802. Loan Discount	%	to
803. Appraisal Fee		to
804. Credit Report		to
805. Lender's Inspection Fee		to
806. Flood Certification Fee		to
807. Tax Service Fee		to
808.		
809.		
810.		
811.		

900. ITEMS REQUIRED BY LENDER TO BE PAID IN ADVANCE

901. Interest From	to	@ 3	/day
902. MIP Totlns. for LifeOfLoan	for	months to	
903. Hazard Insurance Premium for	1.0 years to		
904.			
905.			

> Since closing is the first of the month there isn't any interest to be prepaid.

1000. RESERVES DEPOSITED WITH LENDER

1001. Hazard Insurance	3 months @ $ 250 per month		750
1002. Mortgage Insurance	months @ $ per month		
1003. City/Town Taxes	months @ $ per month		
1004. County Taxes	3 months @ $ 225 per month		675
1005. Assessments	months @ $ per month		
1006.	months @ $ per month		
1007.	months @ $ per month		
1008.	months @ $ per month		

1100. TITLE CHARGES

1101. Settleme	
1102. Abstract	
1103. Title Exa	
1104. Title Insu	
1105. Documen	
1106. Express	
1107. Attorney'	
(inclu	
1108. Title Insurance	to
(includes above item numbers:	
1109. Lender's Coverage	$
1110. Owner's Coverage	$
1111.	
1112.	
1113.	

> As a buyer, your lender will want to keep a reserve (sort of like a prepayment) of real estate taxes and insurance. This will be the start of your escrow account.

1200. GOVERNMENT RECORDING AND TRANSFER CHARGES

1201. Recording Fees: Deed $	; Mortgage $	; Releases $		
1202. City/County Tax/Stamps: Deed		; Mortgage		
1203. State Tax/Stamps: Revenue Stamps 1,400		; Mortgage 525	525	1,400
1204.				
1205.				

1300. ADDITIONAL SETTLEMENT CHARGES

1301. Survey	to		
1302. Pest Inspection	to		
1303.			
1304.			
1305.		1,950	13,400

| 1400. TOTAL SETTLEMENT CHARGES (Enter on Lines 103, Section J and 502, Section K) | | | 0.00 | |

By signing page 1 of this statement, the signatories acknowledge receipt of a completed copy of page 2 of this two page statement.

Settlement Agent

Need more info for buying that perfect home? Read on...

Okay, you've decided to purchase a home. Condo? Town home? Or perhaps a single -family residence. What? You didn't realize there was more than one kind. Let me help you. Each type of housing has its own particular characteristics. What part of the country you live in will also factor into the housing that is available to you. I live in a small town in Florida where the tallest housing allowed is 35 feet. We definitely do not have skyscraping condos. If I travel 3 hours south to Miami, everywhere you look there are mega-tall condos. In Miami, single family residences are only affordable by the Hilton sisters.

Let's look at the advantages and disadvantages of the three housing types.

Single Family Home

Advantages	Disadvantages
Resale value is generally highest on single family homes.	Single family homes are generally more expensive than condos and town homes.
Your place is your own space. If you want to knock down a wall, you can. If you want to plant an orange tree, you can.	All repairs and maintenance costs are yours.
Usually there are no homeowners fees as there are charged with condos and town homes. Gated communities, of single family homes, are an exception to this statement.	Unless a gated community, no amenities such as clubhouse, community pool or security systems. All landscaping is your responsibility.

Condominiums

Advantages

You will be responsible for little or no exterior maintenance or repairs.

Many condominium communities have pools, exercise facilities, saunas, tennis courts for their residents to use. Single family homes offer these amenities less often.

Condominiums are usually priced more affordable than single family homes.

Disadvantages

Condominium communities usually have more restrictions ie: pets, age −55+, RV parking.

You will be responsible for payment of homeowner's association fees.

The inside of your condo is yours, anything beyond your interior walls is owned jointly with the other condominium owners.

Townhouses

Advantages

You own the land that lies beneath the home you own.

Many townhouse complexes have pools, exercise facilities, saunas, tennis courts for their residents to use. Single family homes offer these amenities less often.

Townhouse offer perceived security with neighbors close by.

You will have limited responsibility for exterior repairs and maintenance.

Disadvantages

Townhouse offer owners less privacy than single family homes.

You will be responsible for paying homeowners association fees.

Resale value of a town house is usually less than a single family home.

Town house complexes also usually have more restrictions ie: pets, age −55+, RV parking.

As "gated" communities become increasingly popular, homeowners' association fees (HOA) are also becoming more common. Make sure you know what you're paying for. Usually for condominiums and town house developments, the HOA fees include building insurance. In single-family home gated communities, the HOA fees will not include insurance coverage for your home's structure. Keep this in mind when comparing prices. General rule, more amenities equals higher HOA fees . Think you want immediate access to a golf course, clubhouse, tennis court, pool, boating facility and park? Think again. The price tag for these amenities may turn out to be more than your mortgage payment.

Now you have an idea of what types of housing are available. The next step is to determine how much house you can afford. This step is followed by the actual home search in the neighborhood in which you'd like to live Both of these steps are best accomplished by using the internet.

First pre-qualify your purchase. This step is easily done by typing into a Google search for pre-qualify mortgage calculator. Click onto the sites that are displayed and complete the information boxes. Try to be as honest as possible when completing the boxes. If you are, then you'll have a real number for the amount of house you can afford.

Now, with number in hand, start another Google search. Type the city and state and "Houses for Sale". This search will produce a bunch of listings mostly from realtors. Enter their sites. Most realtor sites will have an icon for MLS . MLS (Multiple Listing Service) is a real estate service that combines the listings for all available properties in an area, except For-Sale-By-Owner (FSBO) properties, in one directory or database.

Online search is a great way to view potential house selections without having to actually spend the time to visit each prospect. Just click on the MLS icon and enter your housing parameters. Thumbnails of each house will be displayed giving you a chance to see pictures of the home. Some listings will provide a virtual tour to give you a better feel for the home. The MLS listing also provides features of the home such as square feet, number of bedrooms, flooring, any views, HOAs, and year built.

Keep track of the homes you like. Once you've finished your review, call the listing realtors to schedule appointments to visit your choices. you will save hours of unnecessary trips to homes that, had you been able to preview, you never would have visited.

Many people are stepping outside the box and considering purchasing a home that is for sale buy owner. What does that mean? Basically, the seller of the home is not using a realtor to attract buyers but instead is self promoting. What does that mean to you as the prospective buyer of a "For Sale Buy Owner" (FSBO) house?

1 - You'll need an attorney to help you with the closing.

2 - You should get a better deal on the home since you won't have to pay those high realtor fees. Normally, a FSBO seller lowers his price to attract buyers away from similar houses that are charging a realtor commission.

If I may be so blunt as to say that I am amazed how much a realtor can make on a simple house sale. Now I know a lot of realtors are saying "There is no such thing as a simple house sale". Take my little town of Vero Beach, Florida. A few years ago, the average price of a home was about $ 300,000. 00. The standard realtor commission to sell that home was 6% of the home's selling price. That's $ 18,000. 00. Now the average price of a home in Vero is over $400,000. 00. Still using 6% as the realtor's commission, the fee is at least $24,000. That's $6,000 more and for what? Did the realtor have to work any harder?

How do you find homes that are for sale by owner? Well, you can take the traditional approach and drive in your desired neighborhood looking for signs posted. This works except for homes that are located in gated communities. Another good option is to go on-line and type in www. buyowner.com. Your computer screen will pull up a selection of criteria to narrow down your focus. This is very similar to using the MLS service.

If you purchase a home that is FSBO, you will need to retain an attorney to draft the Offer and Purchase Contract. These fees will be considerable less than the 6% the realtor charges. Even though the realtor commission comes out of the sellers proceeds, we know who is really paying for this cost.

Well, apparently, many other people have figured out this windfall and have become realtors. Fortunately, this has caused significant competition between realtors, forcing them to reduce their commission rate. You may want to check and see if this situation has occurred in your area. Don't just assume that all realtors charge the same commission rate.

Congratulations, you've cooked another asset!

Garlic Mashed Mortgages
"Applying for a Mortgage"

> Even commitment phobic people will want to be locked in by a commitment letter from a lender!

The dream of the older generation was to pay off a mortgage. The dream of today's young families is to get one. Funny and True! Home prices have been on a huge upward trend and so have mortgages.. This likely means you'll be borrowing more money to get that dream home. That can be intimidating, If you know what your options are, you'll be more confident in your selection.

Garlic Mashed Mortgages
"Applying for a Mortgage"

Ingredients

Bank or mortgage broker =lender

Uniform residential loan application

Survey of the property & appraisal

Application fee or origination fee

Approval !!

Commitment letter

The mortgage document

Preparation

1. Submit an offer letter to purchase your dream house. Make sure that your offer letter states the purchase of the home is contingent on obtaining a mortgage. This is called a financing contingency. This is a pretty standard practice when purchasing or selling a home.

2. Find a banker or mortgage broker to assist you in securing a loan. If one lender turns you down, go to another one. Although most lenders use the same basic information, they may interpret it differently.

3. Complete the Uniform Residential Loan Application. Don't be scared of this form! Go section by section and provide the information requested. If you are unsure of any items, ask your banker/mortgage broker to help you. Their job is to present your information in the best light possible.

4. Review the Commitment Letter– make sure the interest rate , the amount to be financed, and the terms are all correct. Sometimes, bank s will put crazy conditions within their commitment letters ie: you have to keep as a reserve a certain amount of cash (above what you are already putting down).

Recipe's Financial Nutritional Value
30=Degree of Risk
60=Long Tem Value or Growth Potential
10=Income Producing
40=Tax Savings

Sample Portion of a Truth and Lending Statement

TRUTH IN LENDING DISCLOSURE STATEMENT

Creditor	Applicant(s)
ABC Lending Company 123 Lender Street Hometown, USA 99999	The Financial Chef 123 Main Street Hometown, USA 99999
Mailing Address	Property Address 123 Easy Street Happytown, USA 11111
Loan	Preparation Date 01-26-08

> YIKES! This is the total amount of interest that you will pay over the life of the loan. It's more than the amount you borrowed!

ANNUAL PERCENTAGE RATE The cost of your credit as a yearly rate.	FINANCE CHARGE The dollar amount the credit will cost you.	Amount Financed The amount of credit provided to you or on your behalf.	Total of Payments The amount you will have paid after you have made all payments as scheduled.
E 6.2920 %	ES 268,651.34	ES 218,995.33	ES 487,646.67

PAYMENT SCHEDULE:

NUMBER OF PAYMENTS	* AMOUNT OF PAYMENTS	MONTHLY PAYMENTS ARE DUE BEGINNING	NUMBER OF PAYMENTS	* AMOUNT OF PAYMENTS	MONTHLY PAYMENTS ARE DUE BEGINNING
359	1,354.58	02-01-2008			
1	1,352.45	02-01-2036			

> If this box is checked your interest rate can change. If this box is left unchecked than you are guaranteed the same interest rate over the life of the loan.

* Includes mortgage insurance premiums, excludes taxes, hazard insurance or flood insurance.

DEMAND FEATURE: √ This loan does not have a Demand Feature.   This loan has a Demand

ITEMIZATION: You have a right at this time to an ITEMIZATION OF AMOUNT FINANCED.
I/We [ ] do √ do not want an itemization.

REQUIRED DEPOSIT:
[ ] The annual percentage rate does not take into account your required deposit.

VARIABLE RATE FEATURE:
[ ] This loan has a Variable Rate Feature. Variable Rate Disclosures have been provided to you earlier.

SECURITY: You are giving a security interest in:

ASSUMPTION: Someone buying this property
√ cannot assume the remaining balance due under original mortgage terms.
[ ] may assume, subject to lender's conditions, the remaining balance due under original mortgage terms.

FILING / RECORDING FEES: S

PROPERTY INSURANCE:
√ Property / hazard insurance is a required condition of this loan. Borrower may purchase   table to the lender.
Hazard insurance [ ] is [ ] is not available through the lender at an estimate   with term

> Try to stay away from any potential penalties if you pay off your mortgage early.

LATE CHARGES: If your payment is more than   days late, you will be charged   payment.

PREPAYMENT: If you prepay this loan in full or in part, you
[ ] may √ will not have to pay a penalty.
[ ] may √ will not be entitled to a refund of part of the finance charge.

See your contract documents for any additional information regarding non-payment, default, required repayment in full before scheduled date, and payment refunds and penalties.
E means estimate.

I/We hereby acknowledge reading and receiving a complete copy of this disclosure. I/We understand there is no commitment for the creditor to make this loan and there is no obligation for me/us to accept this loan upon delivery or signing of this disclosure.

_____ Date   _____ Date

_____ Date   _____ Date

GENESIS 2000, INC. * V9.3/W11.0 * (818) 223-3260   Form RegZD (03/95)

More about mortgages. Read on...

You've fallen in love with a three bedroom, 2+ 1/2 bath lakefront house, but you've also fallen in love with a four bedroom ranch home complete with a horse barn. The horse barn house is $ 400,000 and the lakefront house is $ 300,000. You have saved $ 65,000 (you've clipped a lot of coupons) for the down payment.

Watch out for PMI Insurance (Private Mortgage Insurance).

Let's compare each option and figure out what the mortgage amounts would be. With the horse barn house, your mortgage would be $335,000 and with the lakefront house, your mortgage would be $235,000.

Watch out for PMI Insurance (Private Mortgage Insurance).

Beware though, not only will your mortgage be more with option #1 but you will be required to have PMI coverage. What is PMI coverage? Private Mortgage Insurance. Basically, if your down payment on a home is less than 20 percent of the appraised value or sales price, you must obtain private mortgage insurance. PMI fees vary depending on the size of the down payment and the loan, but they typically amount to one-half of 1 percent of the loan. In your case, falling in love with the horse barn house would cost you an extra $1,675. 00 each year. I know, now you're thinking, " But it's a beautiful view from that lake front house".

Let's make sure you really know what a mortgage is. Many people think a mortgage is the ball and chain of their existence. Well, that's understandable. You work your whole life to pay off your mortgage. Today, the terms mortgage and mortgage loan are interchangeable. To understand what a mortgage really is, lets discuss what makes up a mortgage.

Simply stated a mortgage contains the following ingredients:

- Principal = amount you have borrowed
- Interest= the charge you incur for borrowing
- Term=the amount of time you are borrowing the money for
- Mortgage Deed = the legal document establishing a loan on property.

The mortgage deed is filed with your county to secure the lender's interest in the property until the loan has been paid off.

If you know the amount, rate and term of your loan, you can go on-line and do a google search for "mortgage calculator". Your search will display websites that will calculate your monthly payment. Some of those sites will also ask you what the monthly insurance and real estate tax payment will be. Most banks now require you to pay these along with your mortgage payment. This is called the escrow portion of your mortgage payment.

When you are required to make an escrow payment, make sure you check the bank's or lender's calculations. I have seen banks incorrectly record insurance and real estate tax assessments.

Although the bank is actually making your insurance payment, you will still receive from your insurance company a copy of your homeowner's policy and a copy of the invoice. Don't pay the invoice! Just check to make sure it agrees with what the bank paid.

Same situation holds true for your real estate taxes. You'll still receive from the county a copy of your property's tax assessment. Don't pay the invoice! Do make sure that the bank has paid the assessment in November. Paying in November entitles you to the greatest discount off your tax bill. The bank should pay the amount in November since they have been charging you monthly throughout the year. If the lender screws up and doesn't pay the bill on time, it shouldn't be at your expense. They should eat the difference.

Now, let's review the different types of mortgage loans that are available.

The easiest way for me to identify the various financing types is to split them into two categories:

1. **Female Financing Types**
2. **Male Financing Types**

Let's start with the male financing types. What characteristics do men seem to have in common? I bet your answers included descriptions such as "fixed" or "unchanging". Sorry guys!

But if the shoe fits... The male mortgage is the fixed rate mortgage. A fixed mortgage has a constant (fixed) interest rate for the entire term of the loan and therefore, has the same payment from month to month. Good news guys! You are the most popular!

Now, turning to the female financing types. What characteristics do women seem to have in common? I bet your answers included descriptions such as "changing" or "unpredictable" or "adapting". The female mortgage is the variable rate mortgage.

A variable or adjustable rate mortgage is one that the interest rate and payments are adjusted to fluctuate with market conditions. If the federal government raises interest rates, then your adjustable rate mortgage should also rise. Same holds true for decreases in interest rates. This makes your payment amounts in a variable rate mortgage very unpredictable at times. Yes, it's true. I am saying that women can be unpredictable or volatile. Sorry girls!

Due to this risk, the adjustable rate mortgage isn't as prevalent as the fixed rate mortgage. Unless you have a strong feeling that interest rates will be on a downward trend in the future, you may want to avoid the volatility of this female mortgage.

So why would anyone want to sign up for the variable or adjustable rate mortgage? The adjustable rate mortgage (ARM) initial interest rate is lower than its counterpart, the fixed rate mortgage. The interval (time period) in which the interest rate of the ARM is adjusted to reflect the current market conditions will vary from lender to lender. Some lenders will offer a "cap" which puts a limit on how many times in a year, the mortgage is allowed to be adjusted.

How much lower the ARM interest rate is when compared to the fixed interest rate will help you determine how desirable an ARM mortgage will be. Also, if you are not planning to live in your home for very long, the variable rate mortgage may be the way to go.

Talk with your banker or mortgage broker about these options and listen to their advice. They should be more up to date with current market trends and predictions.

Congratulations, you've cooked another asset!

IRA Imperial

"Opening an IRA Account"

> Every year contribute to the same IRA account, try not to open a new account each year. With one account is easier to keep track of what you have and you'll save on custodial fees.

With the future of social security benefits in question, IRAs may become the premier provider of retirement income. Unlike social security benefits, IRAs allow you to control how you invest your money. You can invest in low risk certificates of deposit or higher risk stocks and bonds. The choice is yours, not the government's!

IRA Imperial
"Opening an IRA Account"

Ingredients

Money for the initial deposit

Bank, credit union, on-line brokerage company

Application to open IRA

Social security number

Earned income

Preparation

1. Take ingredients to either bank, credit union or online .
2. Ask one of the bank tellers to direct you to who handles opening IRA accounts or click the "New Account" icon on your computer.
3. Inform the new account rep that you would like to open an IRA account. If online follow the step by step instructions.
4. Choose whether you want to open a Traditional, Roth or Educational IRA.
5. Provide the money for the initial deposit. If online mail a check to brokerage company.
6. Name a beneficiary.
7. Request copies of all forms you have signed.
8. Review your monthly IRA statement to see how you're doing.

Recipe's Financial Nutritional Value
20=Degree of Risk
30=Long Tem Value or Growth Potential
10=Income Producing
30 =Tax Savings

Sample IRA Distribution Form

Cook Your Assets Brokerage Company

IRA Distribution Form

Please Print

These are all reasons for taking money out of your IRA account.
Check the appropriate box that applies to you.

Name (Please Print)	Account Number
Address	Date of Birth
	( )
City State Zip	Daytime Telephone Number

This form is being used to effect a distribution from my ❏ Traditional ❏ Roth ❏ Simple ❏ SEP
What kind of distribution would you like? (please check only one)

❏ Premature (I'm under 59½)
❏ Premature Exception Applies (refer to IRS publication 590)
❏ Regular (I'm between 59½ and 70½)
❏ Excess Contribution: Approximate date of excess contribution: _____
An excess contribution in a SEP IRA automatically becomes your IRA contrib... excess occurred.
Have you filed for an extension on your taxes? ❏ Yes ❏ No Extension Date: ___

❏ Death: Decedent's Name: _____ Relationship to D...
You must provide a certified copy of the decedent's Death Certificate. A photoco...
❏ Disability: *You must attach a letter from your physician, verifying the disability...months.*
❏ Mandatory (I am 70½ or older). Please base calculations on (please check one)
❏ A certain number of years _____ (cannot exceed your life expectancy)
❏ My life expectancy alone
❏ My joint life expectancy with my beneficiary
Beneficiary's Name: _____ Relationship: _____ Date of Birth: _____

> Early distributions normally incur a penalty charge. Exceptions may apply if the distribution is made for expenses related to first home purchase, medical, higher education and health insurance premiums.

2   How much would you like to receive? *(please check only one)*

❏ Please distribute $ _____ from fund # _____
❏ Please close my account.
❏ Mandatory distribution as specified above.

3   Do you want us to withhold 10% of the funds toward taxes? ❏ Yes ❏ No

Please read the Notice Withholding on the reverse. Withholding does not apply to the removal of excess contributions, provided the excess is removed by tax filing date for the year in which the excess occurred. If no election is made, we will automatically withhold 10%.

4   When would you like to receive these distributions? *(please check only one)*

❏ As soon as possible.
❏ Monthly on the 15th
❏ Quarterly on the 15th (Jan., Apr., Jul., Oct.)
❏ Annually on the 15th of _____
Please note: Distributions by direct deposit must be $50.00 or greater per fund.

5   Where would you like us to send these distributions? *(please check only one)*

❏ Please transfer to my (non-IRA) Cook Your Asset Account Number _____
❏ Please send to the address on my account.
❏ Please wire to my bank, a voided check is attached.
❏ Please use Direct Deposit to send my bank on a regular basis, a voided check is attached.

Notice of Withholding on Distributions

The distribution you receive from your Cook Your Assets IRA are subject to Federal Income tax withholding, unless you elect not to have withholding apply. You may elect not to have withholding apply to your distributions by checking the "no" box on the other side. Be sure to sign and date the form.

If you elect not to have withholding apply to your distribution, or if you do not have enough Federal Income tax withheld, you may be responsible for payment of estimated taxes. You may incur penalties under the estimated tax rules, if your withholding and estimated tax payments are not sufficient.

Based on the type of distribution you have selected in Section I on the front, it is your responsibility to determine the correct amount of tax due based on all IRA accounts you may own.

Please Note:
If you do not live in the U.S., the distributions are subject to w   ibutions.

You may change your election in the future, by completing and   oke it.

I certify under penalty of perjury, that my Social Security Num

> Generally, distributions are included in gross income and subject to income tax. You may want to consider having federal tax withholding taken on your IRA distribution to avoid any potential penalties.

_____

Signature

_____

Signature Guarantee Stamp

A Signature Guarantee is required only if:
* You are a beneficiary taking a death distribution.
* Your check is to be sent to an address other then the address on record.

You may have your signature guaranteed by a commercial bank, savings bank, credit union, a trust company or a member of a national securities exchange. An acceptable signature must contain the words "signature guaranteed" and the institution's name.

Important Notice for Roth, Simple and SEP IRA Holders

Roth IRA:
Distributions from a Roth IRA which are attributable to either converted amounts or earnings may be taxed as ordinary income and subject to a 10% early withdrawal penalty unless certain requirements are met.

Simple IRA:
Distributions from a Simple IRA prior to age 59 1/2 and within the first two years of participating in an employer's Simple IRA Plan may be subject to a 25% withdrawal penalty.

SEP IRA:
Per IRS Regulation 4972, an excess contribution in a SEP IRA automatically becomes your IRA contribution for the year in which the excess occurred. The amount of excess stated on this form will be coded as your regular (non-SEP) IRA contribution. Should this IRA contribution result in an excess in your regular (non-SEP) IRA, you may remove the IRA excess by submitting a written request attached to this form.

What type of IRA should I get? Read on ...

Let's start with a little history lesson. The IRA account was born out of a need for a retirement plan for people not covered by a company pension plan. It further developed to allow those middle -income individuals to have both a company sponsored retirement plan and an IRA. Since its inception, the amount you can contribute has steadily increased from the original maximum funding of $2,000.

There are different types of IRA accounts. Traditional and Roth IRAs are among the most common. Whether it is beneficial to start a Traditional or Roth IRA depends on your particular circumstances. Below are strengths and weaknesses of the two retirement accounts.

TRADITIONAL IRA

Strengths

- General Rule- you can deduct your annual contributions.
- Interest and Dividends accrue tax- free until you start making withdrawals.

Weaknesses

- Can't make contributions past the age of 70 ½.
- If you or your spouse is covered by a retirement plan at work, your contribution may be limited or even prohibited. The exact allowable amount(s) is a function of your income level(s).
- You or your spouse needs to have earned income in order to make a contribution.
- Withdrawals from your account are generally taxable.

ROTH IRA

Strengths

- Interest and Dividends accumulated tax -free.
- Distributions from Roth IRAs are tax-free until you've withdrawn all your regular contributions.
- You can make contributions at any age, even after reaching 70 ½.

• You can leave your money in your Roth account as long as you live. IRS doesn't require minimum distributions at any age.

Weaknesses

• No immediate tax savings when you make a contribution.
• You or your spouse needs to have earned income in order to make a contribution.
• If you make too much money you will not be able to contribute to a Roth IRA. Ask your tax professional for income specific income levels.

Characteristics common to both Traditional & Roth IRAs

• You must have earned income for the year in order to contrib ute. Dividends, interest, or social security benefits do not qualify as earned income. Wages, compensation, and commissions do qualify.
• Contributions must be in cash. You can take your cash and purchase a stock; that's okay. The initial funding must be done in cash.
• Contributions must be made by the tax-filing deadline. If they are made later, the money will count towards the next filing season.
• Generally, each has the same maximum contribution amounts. (Certain exceptions do apply with each)
• Most distributions before the owner reaches the age of 59 ½ will be subject to an "early withdrawal penalty" equal to 10% of the amount of the distribution.
• If you have a non-working spouse, he or she can contribute to an IRA as long as the two of you combined make as much in annual income as you contribute.

Congratulations, you've cooked another asset!

Iron Skillet Investments

"Opening an Online Brokerage Trading Account "

Using a online trading account, you can buy and sell stocks and mutual funds with just a few key stokes. Commissions or transaction fees are normally lower than placing a stock purchase through the traditional stock broker.

One day the stock market soars a hundred points , the next day the price plunges. Is there a way to predict what the stock market will do? Many people spend their whole lives trying to find a consistent way to forecast stock market movement. Here's a few bizarre indicators that are used to predict the stock market's future. One is the beer index, higher beer sales in the country equals a higher stock market. The hem line index states the higher the hem line, the higher the stock market will be. So ladies showing more leg is a good thing! The Super bowl index, a long time favorite, states that if a NFC team wins then the stock market will be looking up and if a AFC teams wins, then the stock market will start to sliding into a bear market.

Iron Skillet Investments

"Opening an Online Brokerage Trading Account "

Ingredients

Computer preferable with DSL service

Application– online or via mail

$8- Minimum deposit amount

Social security number

Preparation

1. *Decide how much money you want to start trading with. This will be your deposit amount. Most online brokerage companies have minimum deposit guidelines.*

2. *Compare different companies that provide online trading accounts E-trade, Ameritrade, Schwab, and Scottrade are some. Check out www.brokersadvisor.com for comparison reviews of top online brokerage companies.*

3. *Complete the application on line or get a hard copy and send through the mail. You will be asked basic personal information. You must decide what type of account you want; individual, joint, or IRA.*

4. *Send a check or wire transfer for the initial deposit.*

5. *Go online to the web address of your new trading account. Set up a login and a password.*

6. *Make your first online trade. The two basic trades are market trades and limit trades. Market trades purchase your stock at the prevailing asking price. Limit trades allow you to specify what price you would like to purchase at. Your trade will be executed if the asking price equals the price you specified in your limit order.*

7. *Review your monthly online brokerage statement to see how your stocks are performing.*

Recipe's Financial Nutritional Value
20=Degree of Risk
30=Long Tem Value or Growth Potential
10=Income Producing
30 =Tax Savings

Sample Portion - Brokerage Statement

Cook Your Assets Brokerage
123 Financial Boulevard
Hometown, USA 99999

PREPARED FOR:
The Financial Chef
123 Main Street
Hometown, USA 99999

For the period February 1 through February 28, 2008

Acct# 001-234-0007

Portfolio Summary

Investment	Current Value	Prior Value	Period Change	% Change	Estimated Income	Estimated Yield	Portfolio Allocation	Portfolio Allocation
Cash	$.	$.	$.		$.			
MMDA	10,635.41	10,643.17	(6.76)	(0.1)%			8.1%	
Money Market								
Short balance								
Stocks	16,583.73	16,476.79	106.94	0.6%	12.68	0.1%	60.9%	MMDA
Short stocks								
Bonds								
Options								
Short options								
Mutual funds								
Other								
Total	$27,220.14	$27,119.96	$100.18	0.4%	$12.68	0.0%	100%	

This is the prior month's value of each type of investment

This column shows what percentage each asset type comprises in your total portfolio (account).

Cash Activity Summary

	Current	YTD
Opening balance	$ 0.00	$.
Securities purchased	.	.
Securities sold	8.35	8,428.10
Funds deposited	.	.
Funds disbursed	.	.
Income	1.40	4.32
Expense	(20.00)	(20.00)
Other	10.25	(8,412.42)
Closing balance	$ 0.00	$0.00

Income & Expense Summary

	Taxable	Non-Taxable	YTD
Income			
Dividends	$1.40	$.	$4.32
Interest	.	.	.
Other	.	.	.
Expense			
Interest	.	.	.
Fees		(20.00)	(20.00)
Other	.	.	.
Net	$1.40	(S20.00)	($15.68)

Performance Summary

	YTD
Cost basis as of - 2-28-08	$4,101.16
Unrealized gains	.
Unrealized losses	(1,264.80)
Funds deposited/(disbursed)	.
Income/(expense)	(15.68)
Securities received/(delivered)	0.00

This section shows both the current and ytd activity in the cash part of your account. The balance in this account normally is zero. Any excess cash fund should be invested in a money market account.

An unrealized loss becomes real when you sell the stock. Had these stocks been sold at the end of the month, these losses would have been real.

Income Summary Detail

Description	Current	Year to Date
Ordinary Dividends	$ 0.40	$ 0.40
QUALIFIED DIVIDENDS	1.00	2.92
MMDA Interest	3.49	7.95

Account Positions

Investment Description	Symbol/CUSIP	Quantity	Current Price	Market Value	Purchase Date	Cost Basis	Average Cost	Unrealized Gain(Loss)	Annual Income	Yield
Stocks - cash										
Airnet Communications Corp Deleted 10/13/06	ANCCO	200	$ 0.004	$0.80		$.	$ NP	$.	$	
Alcatel Lucent Sponsored Adr	ALU	195	13.25	2,583.75			NP			
California Oil & Gas Corp Com	COGC	1,250	0.56	700.00	08/26/06	1,294.37	1.04	(594.37)		
China Wireless Com	CWLC	4,000	0.0165	66.00	03/10/06	454.90	0.11	(388.90)		
Ciena Corp New Com	CIEN	71	29.16	2,070.36	03/10/06	2,351.80	33.12	(281.44)		
Echostar Comm Corp Cl-A Com	DISH	32	46.53	1,488.96			NP			
Embarq Corp Com	EQ	2	60.04	120.08			NP		5.00	4.2%
Infospace Inc Com	INSP	1	25.66	25.66			NP			
Krispy Kreme Doughnuts Com	KKD	200	9.73	1,946.00			NP			
Lsi Corp Com	LSI	10	8.50	85.00			NP			
Palm Inc Com	PALM	54	16.88	911.52			NP			
Powershares Qoo	QQQC	15	45.96	689.40			NP			
Sirius Satellite Radio Inc Com	SIRI	1,000	2.98	2,980.00			NP			
Sprint Nextel Corp Com	S	46	20.03	921.38			NP			5%
Taser International Inc Com	TASR	200	8.63	1,726.00			NP			
Time Warner Inc Com	TWX	14	20.63	288.82			NP		3.08	1.1%
Total stocks				$16,583.73		$4,101.16		$(1,264.80)	$12.68	0.1%
Total cash account				$16,583.73		$4,101.16		$(1,264.80)	$12.68	0.1%

No amount shown here means your brokerage company doesn't have cost information available for these stocks.

Use these symbols to look up trade information while you are on-line.

It sounds so easy to just start trading...I'm a little scared though, tell me more...

Years ago, you used a stockbroker to buy and sell stocks for you. Commissions used to be a percentage of the purchase or sales price of the stock. If you wanted to buy $1,000 of Exxon stock you may have paid 2% or $20. 00 as a commission. Raise the amount of Exxon stock to $10,000. 00 and you would have paid $200. 00 in commissions. Today, online trading companies charge a flat rate for each trade regardless of dollar value of your stock purchase. Typical fees range from $4 to $15 per stock trade.

Stockbrokers do still exist today. They have felt pressure recently to reduce their commission charges. Not every broker has followed this trend. Perhaps these brokers believe they are justified in charging high fees because with your stock trade you also receive their trading advice. Forgive me again, but let's think logically on this one. Which client is the stockbroker going to spend the most time analyzing and fine- tuning his/her investment portfolio? The answer is the one with the big bucks invested. They'll make more money on commissions. So unless you're pretty wealthy, the stockbroker probably isn't going to give you a whole lot of great advice. I say you're better off paying $8 to $15 for a trade and doing it yourself. This is why this recipe focuses on starting your own online trading account.

Let's start trading.

First, decide how much money you can set aside for investment trading. Calculate all your cash resources. Generally, it's recommended setting aside 3 to 6month worth of cash to have on hand in case of emergencies.

Complete the application and send your deposit to the online brokerage company. In a few days, you'll receive an email with either a password or a pin number to activate your account.

Now let's trade. Purchase a stock first. Each stock will have a bid price and an ask price. I think of the two as a sale price and a retail price. The retail price or ask price is what the seller of the stock wants to get for it. The sales price or bid price is what the buyer wants to pay for it. As buyers, we are always looking for a great sale. Sometimes you can't find that great clearance sale, as is the case if the seller of the stock doesn't want to mark down his stock to equal your bid price.

The seller isn't the only one that influences the stock price. Other buyers and market conditions will have an impact. If the stock is in great demand (many interested buyers) then the ask price probably will go up like generator prices when a hurricane's been forecasted. So when should you buy a generator? The answer is off -season when there isn't much demand. Same principal relates to stock.

Don't always think that the lower the price of a stock, the better. Compare it to this shopping situation. You're browsing through the clearance rack at your favorite department store. You see this beautiful dark chocolate cashmere sweater. You start to push past it. I mean why bother getting your hopes up. Looking at the price tag will only depress you, but you still look anyway. Your heart skips a beat! It's marked $15. 99. "Well, that can't be," you think. "It must be miss marked. I'll ending up waiting in that ridiculously long check out line only to find the price tag should have read $159. 99 not $15. 99. " What the hell, you pluck the sweater from the clearance rack and take your spot in line. A woman in front of you stares at your sweater. You think "Thank god I found it first. What a deal. " Wait,you hear the women saying "I looked at the sweater too but I couldn't get past the big hole at the bottom." "What? A hole?" you think and start to inspect the sweater. And there, sure as day, is a large tear on the bottom of the sweater. "Damn!" you say "It's defective. I knew it was too good to be true. "

Remember this shopping story, when you come across a really cheap stock price. The stock may not be such a great deal but instead it might be defective. Instead of suffering from a huge hole, the stock may be suffering from too little revenues, or too high expenses, or too much debt. Just like the sweater, its price is too good to be true.

The act of purchasing or selling a stock is called an order. Two common types of orders are market and limit. Market orders indicate that the buyer or seller wants the immediate execution of an order at the current market price. There are a few drawbacks with this type of order. First, what if current market price changes from the time you place the order to the time the order is executed? The stock market today changes so rapidly. There is no guarantee what you ask for is what you end up actually getting.

Second, suppose you want to buy a stock at $10. 00, but the current ask price is $12. 00. If you place a market order you'll pay $2. 00 more a share than you wanted to. The alternative is to constantly check the price until it reaches $10. 00 a share. That's way too busy for people with a life. The same holds true in reverse on the sell side. Say you wanted to sell a stock at $12. 00 a share and it's only at $10. 00. Do you really want to lose $2. 00 per share?

Instead of a market order, place a limit order. A limit order indicates the highest price you're willing to pay for a stock , or the lowest price you're willing to sell a stock for. Your order will be executed at the designated price or sometimes even better. This helps protect you from stock market unpredictability.

Same example as above; you want to purchase a stock for $10. 00 a share but it's currently at $12. 00. You place a limit order at $10. 00. The transaction will only happen at a price of $10. 00 or less. Limit orders are GTC – good till cancelled. You may choose the limit order to be good for either for the day or some date in the future. "Till cancelled" means you can delete your order at any time until your price has been reached. The nice feature of a limit order is you can pre-determine a price, execute the order and walk away. You'll be notified if the price reaches your desired level. To me, that's like being notified you won the lottery and not having to play everyday. Limit orders do cost about $5 more than market orders, not a bad trade off for the increased flexibility.

You can also trade mutual funds with your online brokerage account. They are a little different to trade than stocks. Instead of constantly fluctuating prices that stocks experience, mutual funds change their price daily. This price is called the NAV price, net asset value. The fee for buying and selling a mutual fund is usually higher than that of a stock. Fees charged for buying and selling mutual funds are called loads. There are front end and back end loads. Front- end loads are commissions charged when you first purchase the fund. Back end loads are commissions charged when you sell the fund. No -load funds don't charge a commission on the purchase or sale of the fund. There usually is a flat fee of about $40. 00 charged at purchase and sale time.

You can also buy Treasury Bills through your on-line account. You don't have to make a trip to the bank to purchase a Certificate of Deposit anymore. If you are unsure of how to do any of these transactions, you can still actually talk to a representative that will help you.

You can buy and sell stocks and mutual funds all day long but what really counts is your portfolio's performance. One of the great features of online brokerage accounts is the research material available. You can look up charts on a stock's performance, press releases of companies' news and profiles of companies. Each month, you'll receive a statement that summarizes your stocks performances. You can access your online account day or night. So when you can't sleep, you can check out and see how your stocks are performing.

Congratulations, you've cooked another asset!

Disability Insurance with Dill Caper Sauce

" Obtaining Disability Insurance"

> Look for guaranteed insurability as a feature of your disability policy. That way the pounds you gain from future late night potato chip binges won't matter!

Okay, not to be depressing but imagine (god forbid) you suffer a heart attack, car crash, or some other debilitating disease. You wouldn't be able to work. No work means no money. Now, not only do you have to deal with getting well, you also have to deal with going broke. It's not a pleasant thought. Basically, disability insurance provides you money when you are unable to work.

With disability insurance, you would have one less worry during a difficult time.

Disability Insurance with Dill Caper Sauce

" Obtaining Disability Insurance"

Ingredients

Insurance Agent

A job /income

Physical exam (sometimes)

Insurance Quote

Insurance Policy

Preparation

1. First check with your employer to see if they offer disability coverage. You may have coverage and not even know it.
2. Shop for insurance companies that write disability policies. If you have health insurance ask your agent if they quote disability insurance.
3. Complete application/questionnaire for quotes.
4. Review quotes. Ask your agent about "occupational coverage", cost of living adjustment (COLA), term, guaranteed renewable, non-cancelable and elimination periods features.
5. Take a physical if required.
6. Keep signed policy in a secure place.
7. Review your policy yearly. Update your policy for any substantial income changes.
8. Enjoy some peace of mind.

Recipe's Financial Nutritional Value
20=Degree of Risk
30=Long Tem Value or Growth Potential
10=Income Producing
30 =Tax Savings

Sample Disability Application

COOK YOUR ASSETS
DISABILITY INSURANCE COMPANY

1. Personal Information

CHEF	FINANCIAL	THE

Social Security #: ☐ ☐ ☐-☐ ☐-☐ ☐ ☐ ☐

Phone Numbers:

STREET ADDRESS

CITY   ( )   ( )
                                        HOME   WORK

STATE (OR PROVINCE)   ZIP CODE

MEMBER'S DATE OF BIRTH: ___/___/___   **HEIGHT:** ___ft. ___in. **WEIGHT:** ___lbs. **SEX:** ☐ M   ☐ F
                        MO. DAY YEAR

PLACE OF BIRTH: _____
                CITY   STATE

Occupation _____   Major Duties _____

Business Address: _____
                  NUMBER   STREET   CITY   STATE   ZIP
Are you performing the full-time duties of your occupation? (Minimum 30 hours per week)............ ☐ Yes   ☐ No

Gross Annual Income Earned: $ _____

Beneficiary: _____

> Career Plans usually provide benefits up to age 65.
> Five-Year Plans usually provide benefits for a five year time period.

2. Plan Options
Please indicate the Plan options for which you are applying:
a.   **Plan:** ☐ Career Plan ☐ Five-Year Plan
b.   **Waiting Period:** ☐ 90-day   ☐ 180-day
c.   **Benefit Amount:** $ _____ (from $100 to $5,000 per month in $100 units)

3. Other Insurance Information

> The longer the waiting period, the lower the premium.

a. ...come Insurance in force or pending with this or any other company?
   ...w.) .... ☐ Yes   ☐ No
b. ...herein applied for, plus that which will remain in force, or pending in all companies
   ...g from accident or sickness, total more then 60% of monthly earned income?.......... ☐ Yes   ☐ No

Company	Disability Income		To Be Replaced		
	Monthly Benefit	Benefit Period	YES	NO	Date ___/___/___

4. Health Questions
Please answer the following and give details for all "Yes" answers below.

a.   Have you been declined, postponed, modified or rated up for life, accident
     or major medical insurance?.. ☐ No

> Be careful when purchasing more than one disability policy. Duplicate coverage may not be cost efficient. Disclose any existing coverage to your insurance agent so they can provide you with the most appropriate plan.

LH 12401   SIDE

4. Health Questions *continued*

b. Have you ever had high or low blood pressure, stroke, disease or disorder of the heart, blood or blood vessels; mental, anxiety or emotional disorder; diabetes, epilepsy, dizzy spells, chronic or severe headaches; disease or disorder of the nervous system; impaired sight or hearing; liver, kidney or urinary tract disorder; asthma, emphysema, tuberculosis or other respiratory disorder; arthritis, disorder of the neck, back, spine or other musculoskeletal disorder; ulcer or disorder of the digestive system; cancer or tumor; unexplained weight loss in the past 12 months; other illness, disease or injury? .... ☐ Yes ☐ No

c. Have you been diagnosed as having or been treated for Acquired Immune Deficiency Syndrome (AIDS), AIDS Related Complex (ARC) or any other immune deficiency disorder? .... ☐ Yes ☐ No

d. Have you, during the past five years, been disabled, consulted any physician, surgeon, psychiatrist, chiropractor or other practitioner for any reason not mentioned above; or have you been confined or treated in any hospital, sanitarium or similar institution? .... ☐ Yes ☐ No

e. During the past 5 years, have you been counseled, treated or hospitalized for the use of alcohol or drugs? .... ☐ Yes ☐ No

f. Are you currently taking any prescribed medication or receiving or contemplating any medical or surgical treatment? .... ☐ Yes ☐ No

IF YOU ANSWERED "YES" TO ANY OF THE ABOVE, GIVE DETAILS BELOW.
(If you need more space, use a separate sheet.)

Question No.	Complete Details Including Nature of Disorder or Injury	Began Mo./Yr.	Duration	Present Condition	Names and Addresses of Doctors and Hospitals

This next space is usually reserved for "disclaimers" by the disability insurance company. This legal jargon is beyond the scope of our illustration. Each company chooses their own "standard language" presented with a request of the applicant's signature.

Here's more detail on disability insurance features...

It's cold and snowy outside. Rex, your dog, needs to go outside and take care of business. Outside, it's a blizzard. Rex sees a rabbit run across the lawn. He takes off with you in tow, and before you know it, you've tripped, fallen, and broke your leg and fractured your arm. The doctor states that the fracture is in a very unusual place and will take almost a year to heal. You're a physical therapist. Using your hands and arms is a prerequisite.

Six months later, bills have piled up and your arm feels no better. You've tried to apply for Social Security Disability Benefits, but the government says that as long as you can get any job they won't pay. You could be a Burger King cashier, but that won't pay your monthly bills. You can't collect from workers compensation because you weren't injured on the job. You are definitely in a bad situation. This could have been avoided had you purchased an individual disability insurance policy.

Mind you a disability insurance policy won't make you totally whole, but it sure will make life easier in a time when you aren't feeling well to begin with. The average monthly reimbursement is 70% of your income. See the benefit of disability insurance? You're probably thinking "What's the cost?"

Here are some features associated with disability insurance that help determine the price of your premium.

OWN OCCUPATION VS. ANY OCCUPATION:

Take the example above; had you obtained "own occupation" disability insurance, you would have received benefits because you were no longer able to perform the duties of your occupation, physical therapy. Another policy type is "any occupation" disability insurance. With this coverage, your benefits won't start until a doctor declares you unable to work at any job for which you are reasonably qualified.

The premium for "own occupation" coverage is higher than that of the "any occupation". I think of the "any occupation" coverage to be similar to catastrophic health insurance. It provides benefits in the "oh my God!" case of a tragedy. Whether or not you choose the "own occupation" or the "any occupation" feature is a decision of how much coverage you want.

The following are some more terms associated with disability insurance.

GUARANTEED RENEWABLE

Generally speaking this aspect states that your insurance carrier can't cancel you because you've gained some pounds from late night potato chip binges. This holds true for a policy with a NON-CANCELABLE clause. Under these terms, the only way your insurance company can cancel coverage is if they cancel coverage for everyone in your job category.

RESIDUAL BENEFITS

Residual benefits are paid to those who are not 100% disabled. Partial payments are made to those who can't complete all of their job functions.

BENEFIT TERM

Benefit term is the amount of time that your policy will pay benefits. Term options include two years, five years, until retirement, or for life. The longer the term , the higher the premium.

ELIMINATION PERIOD

Elimination period is the time period from when you first get injured to the time you actually start receiving benefits. This feature has a big influence on the amount of your premium. The shorter the elimination period , the higher your premium. Elimination periods vary from 30 days to 120 days. If you have sufficient cash reserves to hold out for a while, do so. The premium difference will make it worth your while.

"COST OF LIVING ADJUSTMENT" (COLA):

"COLA" kicks in additional benefits after a year of disability. It is meant to help you keep up with inflation when you're disabled. Be careful. While a good feature, the extra premium may make it undesirable.

Are there any other ways besides purchasing disability insurance to help you through during a disability? Social Security disability insurance, workers compensation or pension plans are options.

SOCIAL SECURITY

I have to be honest. Please don't rely on Social Security benefits to pull you through a disability. First, the benefits don't start until six months have passed from your injury. Second, the government pays out disability benefits based upon the "any occupation" clause. This clause makes it more difficult for you to collect any benefits.

WORKERS' COMPENSATION

Workers' compensation insurance covers you only if your injury happens at work. The benefits are limited and governed by the state. If you're counting on workers' compensation insurance to protect you, be careful when you're walking your dog Rex or slicing that onion.

PENSIONS

Some government and private companies provide disability benefits in their pension plans. Usually, your pension benefits are reduced by your disability benefits. Thinking of the Enron fiasco, I personally wouldn't want to put all my eggs in that basket.

Congratulations, you've cooked another asset!

Caramelized College Tuition Programs

" Funding College Tuition Programs"

> When was the last time you've seen college costs go down? If you think that the cost to send Little Lucy will be less in the future than a prepaid college plan may not be right for you. If you really believe college costs will decrease in the future, well, I have this Brooklyn Bridge to sell you too!

"Okay, Push, 1,2,3... Now, Breath 1,2,3..." Oh, I can see the head, there it is ! It's coming. Just one last big push! Now come on you can do it! Ready Push!" the doctor coaches. "Ahhhhhhh!",Suzie screams as her bundle of joy falls into the doctor's hands.   Suzie plops back onto her pillow and starts to sob. The nurse concerned, asks Suzie "Are you in pain?" "No" Suzie replies still crying. "Then what's the matter?" the nurse asks. " I was just thinking how much little Elmo's college education will cost!"

Caramelized College Tuition Programs
" Funding College Tuition Programs"

Ingredients

Money

A student– beneficiary

Application fee

Application from the state of your residency

Preparation

Prepaid College Plan

1. *Either access by mail or via internet an application from your state.*
2. *Decide on "Survivor Designation". (Who takes over if you're no longer around)*
3. *Select a tuition plan and local fee plan—choose either 4 yr or 2 yr college attendance.*
4. *Select payment type- lump sum, 5 yr payout or monthly until child starts college.*
5. *Select a dormitory plan– from 1 year up to 5 years. Also, select a payment plan same as in #4.*
6. *Complete application and submit application fee.*

College Investment Plan

1. *Either access by mail or via internet an application from your state*
2. *Decide on "Survivor Designation" (Who takes over if you're no longer around)*
3. *Select investment options—this is the percentage of your contribution allocated to ie: fixed income funds, U.S. equity funds etc.*
4. *Determine if you want to make an initial contribution amount– minimum usually $ 250.00 (varies state to state) or an automatic withdrawal or both.*
5. *Complete application and submit initial contribution if applicable.*

Recipe's Financial Nutritional Value
20=Degree of Risk
50=Long Tem Value or Growth Potential
10=Income Producing
20 =Tax Savings

Sample Portion College Tuition Investment Form

FLORIDA PREPAID COLLEGE PLAN
NEW ACCOUNT APPLICATION

FLORIDA COLLEGE INVESTMENT PLAN
NEW ACCOUNT APPLICATION

IMPORTANT! YOU MAY ENROLL IN THE FLORIDA PREPAID COLLEGE PLAN NOW, BUT YOU WILL BE SUBJECT TO THE PRICES EFFECTIVE OCTOBER 2007. YOU MAY ENROLL IN THE FLORIDA COLLEGE INVESTMENT PLAN YEAR-ROUND.

You may use this application to open a new Florida Prepaid College Plan, a new Florida College Investment Plan or both for the same beneficiary (student). However, you must complete a separate application for each beneficiary. **Please refer to the enclosed Application Instructions.** For information, call 1-800-552-GRAD (4723) or visit www.florida529plans.com.

To enroll online, visit www.florida529plans.com/SignUpToday.

1. TYPE OF ACCOUNT

Select the type of account you are opening: ○ **Prepaid Plan*** ○ Investment Plan

*If you already have a Florida Prepaid tuition plan and want to add a Florida Prepaid local fee plan and/or Florida Prepaid dormitory plan, do **not** use this application. Applications are available at www.florida529plans.com/SignUpToday or call 1-800-552-GRAD (4723).

2. ACCOUNT OWNER

The account owner is the person or entity opening the account. The account owner must be an individual who is a citizen or resident alien of the United States and is 18 years of age or older, or an entity such as a business, organization or trust organized under the laws of the United States. **Indicate whether the account owner is an individual OR a business/organization/trust by completing the appropriate part of Section 2A below.**

A. Individual

❏ Mr. ❏ Mrs. ❏ Ms. ❏ Dr.

Account Owner First Name   MI   Last Name

Account Owner Social Security Number

```
The account owner is the
person/business funding the
account.
```

Business/Organization

Name of Business/Organization

Business/Organization/Trust Tax ID Number

Authorized Representative of Business/Organization/Trust   ❏ Mr. ❏ Mrs. ❏ Ms. ❏ Dr.

First Name   MI   Last Name

* A business, organization or trust must submit additional documentation. Refer to the Application Instructions for the required documentation.

B. Contact Information – Individual Account Owner or Authorized Representative of Business/Organization/Trust

Mailing Address (COMPLETE STREET ADDRESS INCLUDING APARTMENT # OR P.O. BOX)

City   State   Zip Code

Home Telephone   Work Telephone

E-Mail Address

Optional: How did you hear about the program? 1- ❏ I AM A CUSTOMER 2- ❏ FRIEND/FAMILY 3- ❏ WORK 4- ❏ SCHOOL 5- ❏ NEWSPAPER/MAGAZINE 6- ❏ TV 7- ❏ RADIO 8- ❏ FINANCIAL ADVISOR 9- ❏ WEB SITE 10- ❏ OTHER

Optional: Annual Family Income 1- ❏ Under $20,000 2- ❏ $20,000-$29,999 3- ❏ $30,000-$39,999 4- ❏ $40,000-$49,999 5- ❏ $50,000-$69,999 6- ❏ $70,000-$99,999 7- ❏ $100,000 and over

Optional: You are opening this account for? 1- ❏ YOUR CHILD 2- ❏ YOUR GRANDCHILD 3- ❏ OTHER RELATIVE 4- ❏ YOURSELF 5- ❏ OTHER

OFFICE USE: Check/MO #_____ Check/MO $_____ Related AP_____ Other_____ Tracking # 10

PP-06-07 OSAPEP10M   - 1 of 5 -   FORM: FPCB 2006-10

3. SURVIVOR

The survivor becomes the account owner upon death of the account owner in Section 2. The survivor must be an individual who is a citizen or resident alien of the United States and is 18 years of age or older, or an entity such as a business, organization or trust organized under the laws of the United States. The survivor cannot be the same as the account owner. The beneficiary (student) cannot be the survivor unless he/she is 18 years old or older. **Indicate if the survivor is an individual OR a business/organization/trust by completing the appropriate part of Section 3A below.**

A. Individual

Survivor Social Security Number

❑ Mr. ❑ Mrs. ❑ Ms. ❑ Dr.

Survivor First Name

> By naming a survivor, the account will continue even after the death of the original account holder.

Business/Organ...

Business/Organization/Trust Tax ID Number

Name of Business/Organization/Trust

Authorized Representative of Business/Organization/Trust   ❑ Mr. ❑ Mrs. ❑ Ms. ❑ Dr.

First Name   MI   Last Name

* A business, organization or trust must submit additional documentation. Refer to the Application Instructions for the required documentation.

B. Contact Information, if different from the account owner's contact information in Section 2B.

Mailing Address (COMPLETE STREET ADDRESS INCLUDING APARTMENT # OR P.O. BOX)

City   State   Zip Code

Home Telephone   Work Telephone

E-Mail Address

4. BENEFICIARY

The beneficiary is the student who will use the plan.

Beneficiary First Name   MI   Last Name

Beneficiary Social Security Number   Beneficiary Date of Birth

Month   Day   Year

Beneficiary Mailing Address, if different from account owner (COMPLETE STREET ADDRESS INCLUDING APARTMENT # OR P.O. BOX)

City   State   Zip Code

If the beneficiary is a child, mark the age or the grade of the child as of September 1, 2006 below:

a- ❑ Newborn *	b- ❑ Infant **	c- ❑ 1 year old	d- ❑ 2 years old	e- ❑ 3 years old	f- ❑ 4 years old
K- ❑ Kindergarten	1- ❑ First Grade	2- ❑ Second Grade	3- ❑ Third Grade	4- ❑ Fourth Grade	5- ❑ Fifth Grade
6- ❑ Sixth Grade	7- ❑ Seventh Grade	8- ❑ Eighth Grade	9- ❑ Ninth Grade	10- ❑ Tenth Grade	11- ❑ Eleventh Grade

* Newborn: Child born after September 1, 2006.   ** Infant: Child born on/before September 1, 2006, but who is not yet 1 year old.

If the beneficiary is 18 years old or older, or in the 12th grade, provide the projected college enrollment year:

INVESTMENT PLAN ONLY

Optional: Beneficiary Gender   1- ❑ MALE   2- ❑ FEMALE

Optional: Beneficiary Race   1- ❑ WHITE   2- ❑ BLACK   3- ❑ HISPANIC   4- ❑ NATIVE AMERICAN   5- ❑ ASIAN   6- ❑ OTHER

5. FLORIDA PREPAID COLLEGE PLAN ... plete Sections 5A-5D.

> You can choose from 3 different Prepaid College Plans depending on the education plans of the student.

A. Plan Types — Select the type of Prepaid College ... plan below. You may select a different payment option for each plan. Refer to the Enrollment Kit for information about the plan's options.

Tuition Plan – May be purchased for a child who is currently in the eleventh grade or younger.

PLAN TYPE (SELECT ONE): ☐ 4-Year University Tuition Plan   ☐ 2+2 Tuition Plan   ☐ 2-Year Community College Tuition Plan

PAYMENT OPTION (SELECT ONE): ☐ Lump-Sum Payment Plan   ☐ 5-Year Payment Plan (55 monthly payments)   ☐ Monthly Payment Plan (Monthly until child starts college)

Local Fee Plan – May be purchased for a child who is currently in the eighth grade or younger. The local fee plan will automatically be the same type as the tuition plan selected above.

PAYMENT OPTION (SELECT ONE): ☐ Lump-Sum Payment Plan   ☐ 5-Year Payment Plan (55 monthly payments)   ☐ Monthly Payment Plan (Monthly until child starts college)

Dormitory Plan – May be purchased for a child who is currently in the eighth grade or younger.

PLAN TYPE (SELECT ONE): ☐ 1-Year Plan   ☐ 2-Year Plan   ☐ 3-Year Plan   ☐ 4-Year Plan   ☐ 5-Year Plan

PAYMENT OPTION (SELECT ONE): ☐ Lump-Sum Payment Plan   ☐ 5-Year Payment Plan (55 monthly payments)   ☐ Monthly Payment Plan (Monthly until child starts college)

B. Residency Requirement — The beneficiary or the parent/guardian of the beneficiary must have been a Florida resident for the last 12 consecutive months. You **MUST** attach proof of Florida residency to this application.

A COPY of any ONE of the following documents will be accepted:

- Florida driver's license, for the parent listed below, issued at least one year ago. Copy of front and back.
- Proof of full-time Florida employment, for the parent listed below, for the last 12 consecutive months.
- Florida report card or attendance report, for the beneficiary, from the 2005-2006 school year. Current year will not be accepted.
- If the beneficiary is less than 1 year old, a copy of his/her Florida birth certificate.
- Military leave and earnings statement listing Florida as home of record, Florida voter registration card, Florida vehicle registration OR Florida homestead exemption certificate, for the parent listed below, from at least one year ago.

Parent/Guardian First Name   MI   Last Name

NOTE: Divorced parents who are Florida residents applying for their non-resident child must also submit a copy of their divorce decree or the beneficiary's birth certificate.

C. Application Fee — Attach a check or money order for the required application fee. Select ONE of the conditions below and enter an amount to the right. **The application fee is nonrefundable.**

AMOUNT DUE:

$50   STANDARD FEE: Enter $50.00 if the account owner in Section 2 does **not** already have a Florida College Investment Plan for this **same** beneficiary (student).

$ ☐☐.☐☐

OR $30   CURRENT CUSTOMER DISCOUNT: Enter $30.00 if the account owner already has a Florida College Investment Plan for this **same** beneficiary (student), and provide the account number below:

Florida College Investment Plan Account Number

NOTE: Do **not** enter $30.00 if you are also opening a Florida College Investment Plan with this application. If enrolling in both Plans, a discount will be applied on page 4 of this application.

MAKE CHECK OR MONEY ORDER PAYABLE TO: Florida Prepaid College Plan

NOTE: You **cannot** authorize automatic (electronic) payments from a bank account to the Florida Prepaid College Plan with this application. You will receive a separate form once enrolled.

D. Account Owner Authorization and Signature

By signing and initialing below, I certify that (1) all the information provided on this application and on the documentation furnished to the Florida Prepaid College Board with this application is true, complete and correct; (2) I am a citizen or resident alien of the United States, and I am at least 18 years old; (3) if I am signing on behalf of a business, organization or trust organized under the laws of the United States, I am authorized to make these certifications and representations to sign this application on behalf of such business, organization or trust; and (4) the survivor and the beneficiary are citizens or resident aliens of the United States. I further certify, acknowledge and represent as follows:

- I have read and understand the Florida Prepaid College Plan Master Covenant, and consent to the policies, terms and conditions of the Florida Prepaid College Plan and the Master Covenant. I understand that the Florida Prepaid College Plan Master Covenant, which is incorporated into this application by reference, as it relates to enrollment in the Florida Prepaid College Plan, constitutes a legally binding agreement between me and the Florida Prepaid College Board. I understand that the policies, terms and conditions of the Florida Prepaid College Plan and the Master Covenant may be amended from time to time without prior notice, and I understand and agree that I will be subject to those amendments. **INITIALS:** ———

Signature of Account Owner or Authorized Representative of Business/Organization/Trust   Date

Return your application, check or money order, and any required documentation to: Florida Prepaid College Board, P.O. Box 6448, Tallahassee, FL 32314-6448

6. FLORIDA COLLEGE INVESTMENT PLAN
To open a Florida College Investment Plan, complete Sections 6A-6D.

A. Investment Option(s) — Indicate below, in percentages, how you want to allocate your contributions. You may allocate your contributions to one or any combination of the investment options below. Refer to the Disclosure Statement for more information.

INVESTMENT OPTION	ALLOCATION
Fixed Income Investment Option	☐☐☐ %
U.S. Equity Investment Option	☐☐☐ %
Balanced Investment Option	☐☐☐ %
Age Based/Years To Enrollment Investment Option	☐☐☐ %
Money Market Investment Option	☐☐☐ %
	100 % (ALLOCATION MUST TOTAL 100%)

B. Application Fee and Initial Contribution — Attach a check or money order for the following:

1. APPLICATION FEE. **The application fee is nonrefundable.** Select ONE of the conditions below and enter an amount to the right:

$ ☐☐.☐☐

$50 STANDARD FEE: Enter **$50.00** if opening only a **Florida College Investment Plan.**

OR $30 COMBINATION APPLICATION FEE: Enter **$30.00** if opening both a **Florida College Investment Plan** and a **Florida Prepaid College Plan.**

OR $30 CURRENT CUSTOMER DISCOUNT: Enter **$30.00** if this same account owner already has a **Florida Prepaid College Plan** for this same beneficiary (student), and provide the account number below:

☐☐☐☐☐☐☐☐☐☐☐

Florida Prepaid Tuition Plan Account Number

> You have a choice with the College Investment Plan of the type of assets that will be in your account.

2. INITIAL CONTRIBUTION. Enter an initial contribution of at least **$250.00** to the right, **OR** authorize automatic contributions of at least $25 per month in Section 6C. (If authorizing automatic contributions, do not enter amount in boxes to the right.)

+ $ ☐☐☐,☐☐☐.☐☐

AMOUNT DUE: $ ☐☐☐,☐☐☐.☐☐

MAKE CHECK OR MONEY ORDER PAYABLE TO: Florida College Investment Plan

C. Automatic Contributions — To authorize automatic (electronic) contributions from a bank account to the Florida College Investment Plan:

1. **Attach a voided check or pre-printed deposit slip for the bank account from which the automatic contributions are to be withdrawn.**

2. **Select frequency of withdrawals (Select ONE):** ☐ 1st of each month ☐ 15th of each month ☐ 1st and 15th of each month

3. **Provide amount of withdrawal from this bank account each month:** $ ☐☐,☐☐☐.☐☐ ($25 MINIMUM EACH MONTH)

4. Select type of bank account. (Select ONE): ☐ Checking Account ☐ Savings Account

D. Rollovers* — Complete only if you are funding your Investment Plan with a rollover contribution. Mark the type of rollover below:

☐ Another 529 Plan ☐ U.S. Savings Bond ☐ Coverdell Education Savings Account

☐ UTMA/UGMA: If you are funding your account with a transfer from an UTMA/UGMA, mark here to acknowledge that you are the custodian and will maintain this account for the minor beneficiary pursuant to the Uniform Gifts/Transfers to Minors Act in the State of _____.

* Refer to the Application Instructions for the required documentation.

E. Account Owner Authorization and Signature

By signing and initialing below, I certify that (1) all the information provided on this application and on the documentation furnished to the Florida Prepaid College Board with this application is true, complete and correct; (2) I am a citizen or resident alien of the United States, and I am at least 18 years old; (3) if I am signing on behalf of, a business, organization or trust organized under the laws of the United States, I am authorized to make these certifications and representations, and to sign this application on behalf of such business, organization or trust; and (4) the survivor and the beneficiary are citizens or resident aliens of the United States. I further certify, acknowledge and represent as follows:

• I have read and understand the Florida College Investment Plan Disclosure Statement and Participation Agreement, and consent to the policies, terms and conditions of the Florida College Investment Plan and the Participation Agreement. I understand that the Participation Agreement, which is incorporated into this application by reference, as it relates to enrollment in the Florida College Investment Plan, constitutes a legally binding agreement between me and the Florida Prepaid College Board. I understand that the policies, terms and conditions of the Florida College Investment Plan and the Participation Agreement may be amended from time to time without prior notice, and I understand and agree that I will be subject to those amendments. INITIALS: _____

• I understand that enrolling in the Florida College Investment Plan and investing my funds in the investment options involves a high degree of risk, account values may fluctuate and there is no guarantee. I understand that I could lose all funds, including any earnings on those funds, deposited in the account, and investments in the Florida College Investment Plan are not deposits or obligations of, or insured or guaranteed, by the State of Florida, the United States government, the Florida Prepaid College Board, the Federal Deposit Insurance Corporation, or any other governmental agency or financial institution. INITIALS: _____

_____   _____
Signature of Account Owner or Authorized Representative of Business/Organization/Trust   Date

Return your application, check or money order, and any required documentation to: Florida Prepaid College Board, P.O. Box 6448, Tallahassee, FL 32314-6448

Need more details of college investment plans?

Since college tuition programs are state managed, the information I provide may differ from that of your resident state. There are two types of college savings plans: the prepaid college plan and the college investment plan. The IRS likes these plans so much that they attached some tax breaks to each plan. Check with your state to see which plans they offer. Some states offer both plan types.

Florida sponsors both plan types making it easy for me to use my native state as an example. We'll compare the features of a prepaid plan and an investment plan. Use this information as a basis to determine the benefits and disadvantages of your state's program(s). Either call your state's finance office or go online to obtain specific rules and policies for their 529 college plans.

Prepaid College Plans Advantages

1. Financially guaranteed by the State of Florida so you won't lose money.
2. Earnings on qualified withdrawals are exempt from Federal Income Tax.
3. When your child's ready to go to college, you will be paying at today's rate for tuition, local fees and dormitory costs.
4. Can be used at any of the State's public universities and community colleges.
5. Refunds are allowed if you decide not to use the plan.
6. Even if you make monthly payments, your payment amount will remain fixed.

College Investment Plans Advantages

1. Flexibility of investment options.
2. Earnings on qualified withdrawals are exempt from Federal Income Tax.
3. Large contributions are possible. Some State's maximum allowable contributions exceed $250,000.
4. Can be used at most private or public school anywhere in the country.
5. You can withdraw your contributions and earnings at any time (penalties may apply).
6. Low impact for determining whether or not you qualify for financial aid.
7. You can open an account for a child, adult or yourself.

Prepaid College Plans Disadvantages

1. Can only be used only for State sponsored universities and colleges.
2. Rollovers of other college savings plans are not allowed. You cannot rollover your Educational IRA into your Prepaid College Plan.
3. The Prepaid Plan has a more adverse effect when determining whether or not you qualify for financial aid. The beneficiary must be a child in the 11th grade or younger. Either the child or the parent/guardian must be a resident of Florida State.

College Investment Plans Disadvantages

1. The State doesn't guarantee that your investments will make a profit. These are new programs with very little investment history.
2. Certain withdrawals will carry a tax penalty of 10%.
3. The State does not have to report its investment performance on a regular basis.
4. The plan is assessed an administration fee. The fee is usually less than one percent of your account value.

Picture this. You're a single parent who is struggled to save money for your children to go to a State University. What if little Elmo decides he doesn't want to go to the University of Florida? Little Elmo, now 18, wants "to find" himself in Europe. His classroom will be Europe, and his teacher will be life.

You think, "No way, I've saved all this money for your college education!"

Let him go. You still have little Sally. Just transfer the college savings program to little Sally whose much more responsible.

What if it's too late? Say, your child's high school graduation is this year. Check out every possibility for a scholarship or grant. Companies, organizations, individuals all sponsor scholarships and grants. Again, the internet is a great place for researching available scholarships. Often the more obscure the grant, the fewer people will apply.

Financial aid or student loans may also be an avenue. Ask your prospective university for a financial aid applications. Most forms are income generated. The higher you're net worth the less likely you will be approved.

Congratulations, you've cooked another asset!

Refinanced Home Loans with Ranchero Sauce

" Refinancing Your Home"

> One good reason to refinance is to get rid of your PMI (private mortgage insurance). If the value of your house has increased substantially you may have built up enough equity in your home that PMI insurance is no longer required.

Interest rates rise and interest rates fall. This will always be the case. What was once a "good deal" yesterday may not be anymore. When interest rates are falling, people stampede like cattle to their lenders to refinance their home loans. Don't be a follower and do what the rest of the herd does. Look at your own particular situation and review the numbers to make your decision. Keep in mind your lender makes money on a refinance so they may not have your best interest at heart. Follow the recipe below and you can decide for yourself.

Refinanced Home Loans with Ranchero Sauce
" Refinancing Your Home"

Ingredients

Bank or mortgage broker =lender

New appraisal

Misc fees ($$$)

Approval !!

Closing statement

New mortgage document & mthly payment

New escrow account

Preparation

1. Go on-line and google search—Mortgage Calculators. Using same mortgage amount and term , calculate your new payment with your new proposed interest rate. Take your new mortgage amount and subtract it from your old mortgage amount, the resulting amount is your monthly savings.
2. Ask your lender for the prospective fees that will be charged for the refinance. Take that amount and divide it by the amount you will be saving. The resulting amount is how many months until you recover the costs of refinancing.
3. If you plan on staying in your home for as at least the amount of months until you recover the costs of your refinancing, then refinancing is a smart choice. Have your lender start the paperwork process.
4. You'll probably need an updated appraisal. Using the same appraiser as when you first purchased the property will most likely save you money.
5. Sign new paperwork and enjoy your new lower payment!

Recipe's Financial Nutritional Value
10=Degree of Risk
20=Long Tem Value or Growth Potential
40=Income Producing
20 =Tax Savings

Sample of Good Faith Estimate

3. SURVIVOR

The survivor becomes the account owner upon death of the account owner in Section 2. The survivor must be an individual who is a citizen or resident alien of the United States and is 18 years of age or older, or an entity such as a business, organization or trust organized under the laws of the United States. The survivor cannot be the same as the account owner. The beneficiary (student) cannot be the survivor unless he/she is 18 years old or older. **Indicate if the survivor is an individual OR a business/organization/trust by completing the appropriate part of Section 3A below.**

A. Individual

❑ Mr. ❑ Mrs. ❑ Ms. ❑ Dr.

Survivor Social Security Number

Survivor First Name

> By naming a survivor, the account will continue even after the death of the original account holder.

Business/Organization

Business/Organization/Trust Tax ID Number

Name of Business/Organization/Trust

Authorized Representative of Business/Organization/Trust   ❑ Mr.   ❑ Mrs.   ❑ Ms.   ❑ Dr.

First Name   MI   Last Name

* A business, organization or trust must submit additional documentation. Refer to the Application Instructions for the required documentation.

B. Contact Information, if different from the account owner's contact information in Section 2B.

Mailing Address (COMPLETE STREET ADDRESS INCLUDING APARTMENT # OR P.O. BOX)

City   State   Zip Code

Home Telephone   Work Telephone

E-Mail Address

4. BENEFICIARY

The beneficiary is the student who will use the plan.

Beneficiary First Name   MI   Last Name

Beneficiary Social Security Number   Beneficiary Date of Birth

/   /

Month   Day   Year

Beneficiary Mailing Address, if different from account owner (COMPLETE STREET ADDRESS INCLUDING APARTMENT # OR P.O. BOX)

City   State   Zip Code

If the beneficiary is a child, mark the age or the grade of the child as of September 1, 2006 below:

a- ❑ Newborn *	b- ❑ Infant **	c- ❑ 1 year old	d- ❑ 2 years old	e- ❑ 3 years old	f - ❑ 4 years old
K- ❑ Kindergarten	1- ❑ First Grade	2- ❑ Second Grade	3- ❑ Third Grade	4- ❑ Fourth Grade	5- ❑ Fifth Grade
6- ❑ Sixth Grade	7- ❑ Seventh Grade	8- ❑ Eighth Grade	9- ❑ Ninth Grade	10- ❑ Tenth Grade	11- ❑ Eleventh Grade

* Newborn: Child born after September 1, 2006.   ** Infant: Child born on/before September 1, 2006, but who is not yet 1 year old.

If the beneficiary is 18 years old or older, or in the 12th grade, provide the projected college enrollment year:

INVESTMENT PLAN ONLY

Optional: Beneficiary Gender   1- ❑ MALE   2- ❑ FEMALE

Optional: Beneficiary Race   1- ❑ WHITE   2- ❑ BLACK   3- ❑ HISPANIC   4- ❑ NATIVE AMERICAN   5- ❑ ASIAN   6- ❑ OTHER

Is it the right time to refinance?

When is the right time to refinance? The obvious answer is when interest rates are continuously falling. There are other times when refinancing makes sense too.

How much do interest rates have to fall for refinancing to make sense? As my recipe shows, use the internet to help you make a few simple calculations to determine if the time is right. Take the current (lower) interest rate and recalculate your mortgage payment using the same mortgage amount and term. There are many sites that have mortgage calculators to help with this task.

Now subtract the proposed new monthly mortgage amount from the old mortgage amount. This remainder is your estimated monthly savings.

Ask your lender what the total fees will be to refinance (appraisal, points etc.). Your lender should provide you with a form, called a Good Faith Estimate. This form discloses estimates of all the settlement charges likely to be incurred at the time of closing. Use the Good Faith Estimate to calculate the total amount of fees. Divide the monthly savings amount into the total amount of fees. This number is the number of months it will take to recover the cost of refinancing. If you plan on moving from your house before you recover the cost of refinancing, then you lose. To win, you need to stay in your home longer than the period to recover costs is.

Besides capitalizing on a downward trend of interest rates, there are other reasons to refinance.

"SAY GOOD-BYE TO PMI!"

One good reason to refinance is to get rid of your PMI (private mortgage insurance). If the value of your house has increased substantially you may have built up enough equity in your home that PMI insurance is no longer required. Private mortgage insurance is required when you are financing more than 80% of the appraised value of your home. As you pay the mortgage down or if your house's appraised value increases, you build equity in your home. If you build more than 20% equity in your home, PMI insurance will not be required.

"YOU NEED CASH"

Taking cash from your home's equity is another reason to refinance. Let's say you want to build a pool on your property. You could get a home equity loan or you could refinance your home.Compare the interest rates to help you decide which path you want to take. Let's say you need money for your child's college tuition. Refinancing would allow you to take equity out of your home tax free!

"BETTER CREDIT RATING"

People who had lousy credit when they first purchased their home paid higher than average interest rates. If they have cleaned up their credit, they may be able to refinance at a much lower rate. If you fall into this group, have your lender check what interest rate you would qualify for based upon your new credit rating.

Congratulations, you've cooked another asset!

Here's a financial diet tip!
Are you thinking about
refinancing?

Most lenders will require a
current title insurance policy.
You may be able to receive a
reduced rate off the standard
premium charged on the title
insurance policy. You will need to
have kept a copy of your original
title policy in order to qualify.

Ask your mortgage broker if you
qualify for a reissue rate.

Tempura Taxes

" Filing Your Tax Return"

> If your tax return shows a balance due, try not to pay with a credit card. The IRS will access a service charge of up to 2.5 percent of the amount of tax you owe!

You're at a party and you overhear a conversation. "Cool Carl" is trying to impress "Hot Heather". "Boy, I really screwed the IRS this year," he says. "My refund was $5,000!" Carl's thinking "Hot Heather " will be amazed and think he's really smart. You should be thinking "Lord, that Carl's a dumb bunny". You may be asking, "Why should I be thinking that?"

The answer is this. If someone has less taxes withheld from their paychecks during the year, they would have more take home pay each pay period. They could take that extra money and save it, earning interest. Carl's way, the government got to use his money the whole year then giving it back to him when he files his taxes. He didn't earn a dime of interest. Who screwed who?

Tempura Taxes
" Filing Your Tax Return"

Ingredients

Form 1040, or Form 1040A, or Form 1040EZ

Income

Deductions

Software for preparing taxes or a CPA

Preparation

1. *Review your last year's tax return. Refresh yourself and check the return for items that may pertain to this year.*

2. *Gather all your tax documents together. If you are using a paid preparer ask them for a tax organizer. This will provide a basis to work from when gathering your information. Tax software programs like Turbo Tax will provide a checklist to help you organize your information.*

3. *Input your information and process your return. Check for any errors. Most software programs will prompt you to correct any errors. If you are using a paid preparer schedule a meeting to drop off your taxes and go over any questions you may have. DO NOT BE AFRAID TO ASK YOUR PREPARER ANY TYPE OF TAX QUESTION– that's what they are there for. Also, be sure to check the accuracy of your tax return, even paid preparers can make mistakes.*

4. *Print or Electronically File (E File) your tax return. Electronic processing has become increasingly more popular. By E Filing any refund is received quicker and the IRS will provide a confirmation of receipt of your tax return.*

Recipe's Financial Nutritional Value
20=Degree of Risk
30=Long Tem Value or Growth Potential
20=Income Producing
75 =Tax Savings

Sample Pages of Form 1040
for Illustrative Purposes

Form 1040 Department of the Treasury—Internal Revenue Service **2006**

U.S. Individual Income Tax Return (99)

For the year Jan. 1-Dec. 31, 2006, or other tax year beginning , 2006, ending , 20

OMB No. 1545-0074

Label
(See instructions on page 16.)
Use the IRS label.
Otherwise, please print or type.

Your first name and initial: Financial Last name: Chef

Your social security number: 000 00 0000

If a joint return, spouse's first name and initial Last name

Spouse's social security number

Home address (number and street). If you have a P.O. box: 123 Main Street

City, town or post office, state, and ZIP code. If you have: Hometown , USA 99999

> Make sure you enter your social security number correctly. This is how the IRS identifies you.

You must enter your SSN(s) above. ▲

Checking a box below will not change your tax or refund.

Presidential Election Campaign ▶ Check here if you, or your spouse if filing jointly, (16) ▶ ☐ You ☐ Spouse

Filing Status
Check only one box.

1 ☑ Single
2 ☐ Married filing jointly (even if only one had income)
3 ☐ Married filing separately. Enter spouse's SSN above and full name here. ▶
5 ☐ Qualifying widow(er) with dependent child (see page 17)

Exemptions

6a ☑ Yourself. If someone can claim you as a dependent, do **not** check box 6a
b ☐ Spouse
c Dependents:

(1) First name Last name	(2) Dependent's social security number	(3) Dependent's relationship to you	(4) ✓ if qualifying child for child tax credit (see page 19)
			☐
			☐
			☐
			☐

If more than four dependents, see page 19.

Boxes checked on 6a and 6b
No. of children on 6c who:
• lived with you
• did not live with you due to divorce or separation (see page 20)
Dependents on 6c not entered above

d Total number of exemptions claimed

Add numbers on lines above ▶

Income

Attach Form(s) W-2 here. Also attach Forms W-2G and 1099-R if tax was withheld.

If you did not get a W-2, see page 23.

Enclose, but do not attach, any payment. Also, please use Form 1040-V.

7	Wages, salaries, tips, etc. Attach Form(s) W-2	7	100000
8a	Taxable interest. Attach Schedule B if required	8a	1000
b	Tax-exempt interest. **Do not** include on line 8a	8b	
9a	Ordinary dividends. Attach Schedule B if required	9a	
b	Qualified dividends (see page 23)	9b	
10	Taxable refunds, credits, or offsets of state and local income taxes (see page 24)	10	
11	Alimony received	11	
12	Business income or (loss). Attach Schedule C	12	
13	Capital gain or (loss). Attach Schedule D if required	13	-3000
14	Other gains or (losses). Attach Form 4797	14	
15a	IRA distributions 15a	15b	
16a	Pensions and annuities 16a	16b	
17	Rental real estate, royalties, partnerships, S corporations	17	
18	Farm income or (loss). Attach Schedule F	18	
19	Unemployment compensation	19	
20a	Social security benefits 20a	20b	
21		21	
22	Add the amounts in the far right column for lines	22	98000

> For each year, this is the maximum amount of net loss you can deduct for the sale of your investments. What is net loss? Basically, it's the amount your total losses exceed your total gains.

Adjusted Gross Income

23	Archer MSA deduction. Attach Form 8853		
24	Certain business expenses of reservists, performing artists, and fee-basis government officials. Attach Form 2106 or 2106-EZ	24	
25	Health savings account deduction. Attach Form 8889	25	
26	Moving expenses. Attach Form 3903	26	
27	One-half of self-employment tax. Attach Schedule SE	27	
28	Self-employed SEP, SIMPLE, and qualified plans	28	
29	Self-employed health insurance deduction (see page 29)	29	
30	Penalty on early withdrawal of savings	30	
31a	Alimony paid b Recipient's SSN ▶	31a	
32	IRA deduction (see page 31)	32	4000
33	Student loan interest deduction (see page 33)	33	
34	Jury duty pay you gave to your employer	34	
35	Domestic production activities deduction. Attach Form 8903	35	
36	Add lines 23 through 31a and 32 through 35	36	4000
37	Subtract line 36 from line 22. This is your adjusted gross income ▶	37	94000

For Disclosure, Privacy Act, and Paperwork Reduction Act Notice, see page 80. Cat. No. 11320B

Form 1040 (2006)   Page **2**

Tax and Credits	38	Amount from line 37 (adjusted gross		94000
	39a	Check { ☐ **You** were born before if: { ☐ **Spouse** was born befo		
Standard Deduction for—	b	If your spouse itemizes on a separate return o		
	40	**Itemized deductions** (from Schedul		5150
	41	Subtract line 40 from line 38		88850
• People who checked any box on line 39a or 39b or who can be claimed as a dependent, see page 34.	42	If line 38 is over $112,875, or you provided housing to a person displaced by Hurricane Katrina, see page 36. Otherwise, multiply $3,300 by the total number of exemptions claimed on line 6d	42	3300
	43	**Taxable income.** Subtract line 42 from line 41. If line 42 is more than line 41, enter -0-	43	85550
	44	**Tax** (see page 36). Check if any tax is from: **a** ☐ Form(s) 8814 **b** ☐ Form 4972	44	18065
• All others:	45	**Alternative minimum tax** (see page 39). Attach Form 6251	45	
Single or Married filing separately $5,1	46	Add lines 44 and 45 ▶	46	18065
	47	Foreign tax credit. Attach Form 1116 if required	47	
Mar joint Qua wido $10,300	48	Credit for child and dependent care expenses. Attach Form 2441	48	
	49	...led. Attach Schedule R	49	
	50	...863	50	
	51	...credit. Attach Form 8880	51	
	52	... Form 5695	52	
Head of household, $7,550	53	Child tax credit (see page 42). Attach Form 8901 if required	53	
	54	Credits from: **a** ☐ Form 8396 **b** ☐ Form 8839 **c** ☐ Form 8859	54	
	55	Other credits: **a** ☐ Form 3800 **b** ☐ Form 8801 **c** ☐ Form	55	
	56	Add lines 47 through 55. These are your **total credits**	56	
	57	Subtract line 56 from line 46. If line 56 is more than line 46, enter -0- ▶	57	18065
Other Taxes	58	Self-employment tax. Attach Schedule SE	58	
	59	Social security and Medicare tax on tip income not reported to employer. Attach Form 4137	59	
	60	Additional tax on IRAs, other qualified retirement plans, etc. Attach Form 5329 if required	60	
	61	Advance earned income credit payments from Form(s) W-2, box 9	61	
	62	Household employment taxes. Attach Schedule H	62	
	63	Add lines 57 through 62. This is your **total tax** ▶	63	18065
Payments	64	Federal income tax withheld from Forms W-2 and 1099	64	20000
	65	2006 estimated tax payments and amount applied from 2005 return	65	
If you have a qualifying child, attach Schedule EIC.	66a	**Earned income credit (EIC)**	66a	
	b	Nontaxable combat pay election ▶	66b	
	67	Excess social security and tier 1 RRTA tax withheld (see page 60)	67	
	68	Additional child tax credit. Attach Form 8812	68	
	69	Amount paid with request for extension to file (see page 60)	69	
	70	Payments from **a** ☐ Form 2439 **b** ☐ Form 4136 **c** ☐ Form 8885	70	
	71	Credit for federal telephone excise tax paid. Attach Form 8913 if required	71	
	72	Add lines 64, 65, 66a, and 67 through 71. These are your **total payments** ▶	72	20000
Refund Direct depo See page 6 and fill in 74 74c, and 74 or Form 888	73	...line 63 from line 72. This is the amount you **overpaid**	73	1935
	74a	...to you. If Form 8888 is attached, check here ▶ ☐	74a	
		▶ **c** Type: ☐ Checking ☐ Savings		
	75	Amount of line 73 you want applied to your **2007 estimated tax** ▶	75	1935
Amount You Owe	76	**Amount you owe.** Subtract line 72 from line 63. For details on how to pay, see page 62 ▶	76	
	77	Estimated tax penalty (see page 62)	77	

Third Party Designee   Do you want to allow another person to discuss this return with the IRS (see page 63)? ☐ **Yes.** Complete the following. ☐ **No**

Designee's name ▶	Phone no. ▶ ( )	Personal identification number (PIN) ▶	

Sign Here   Under penalties of perjury, I declare that I have examined this return and accompanying schedules and statements, and to the best of my knowledge and belief, they are true, correct, and complete. Declaration of preparer (other than taxpayer) is based on all information of which preparer has any knowledge.

Joint return? See page 17. Keep a copy for your records.

Your signature	Date	Your occupation	Daytime phone number ( )
Spouse's signature. If a joint return, **both** must sign.	Date	Spouse's occupation	

Paid Preparer's Use Only

Preparer's signature ▶	Date	Check if self-employed ☐	Preparer's SSN or PTIN
Firm's name (or yours if self-employed), address, and ZIP code ▶		EIN	
		Phone no. ( )	

Form **1040** (2006)

Annotation: Do you pay state income tax, real estate taxes, high medical bills? Do you make large donations to charity? You may be able to itemize your deductions rather than use the standard deduction. Tell your tax professional about all your expenses.

Annotation: This is a tax usually associated with high income individuals.

Annotation: You may qualify for an additional tax credit if you have three or more children.

Let's Talk More Taxes...

What is tax deductible one year may not be the next. The same holds true in reverse. Keeping updated to tax law changes often is overwhelming to taxpayers. Don't feel too bad, many IRS agents feel the same way. Test your awareness to tax code changes by taking the quiz below.

Is it deductible?

1. Accounting fees for IRS audits?   Yes___ No___
2. Prescription contraceptives   Yes___ No___
3. Appraisal fees forcharitable donations   Yes___ No___
4. Alcoholism and drug-abuse treatment   Yes___ No___
5. Breach of employment contract damages you paid Yes___ No___
6. Mortgage prepayment penalties   Yes___ No___
7. Veterinary bills   Yes___ No___
8. Homeowner's insurance   Yes___ No___
9. Trips to rental property   Yes___ No___
10. Life insurance premiums   Yes___ No___
11. Legal fees paid to secure collection of alimony   Yes___ No___
12. Legal costs to secure child support payments   Yes___ No___
13. Vehicle excise tax   Yes___ No___
14. Homeowners association dues   Yes___ No___
15. IRA custodial fees   Yes___ No___
16. Long -erm care premiums   Yes___ No___
17. Legal costs to protect Social Security payments   Yes___ No___
18. Funeral costs   Yes___ No___
19. Political contributions   Yes___ No___
20. Temporary living expenses (during moving)   Yes___ No___

See how you fared. Score your responses to the answer key below.

Answer Key

1 (Yes) 2 (Yes) 3 (Yes) 4 (Yes) 5 (Yes) 6 (Yes) 7 (No) 8 (No) 9 (Yes) 10 (No) 11

(Yes) 12 (No) 13 (Yes) 14 (No) 15 (Yes) 16 (Yes) 17 (Yes) 18 (No) 19 (No) 20 (No)

Please note that some of the "yes" responses are subject to limitations-contact your tax professionals for further detail.

"Is my spouse deductible?" I have to laugh, to myself of course, each time I'm asked this question. Believe it or not, the taxpayers were totally serious when asking the question. The correct answer is no, although, many would like to argue against this position. I have heard many times from husbands and wives, "Well, I should be able to write him/her off with all the aggravation he/she puts me through!" I always say "You can write them off; you just can't get a tax deduction for it!"

The above list isn't comprehensive to all tax deductions. The quiz is provided to demonstrate that what may appear to be allowable sometimes isn't, and items that you wouldn't have suspected to be write-offs, surprisingly are. Using accurate reference material or a professional tax preparer will increase your odds of capitalizing on the do's and don't's of tax filing.

How would you score an IRS audit?

The average taxpayer probably cannot even answer this question. More importantly, what if you fail? The IRS doesn't grade on a curve, nor does it offer makeup exams. What is the best way to guarantee more positive results? Remember back to your school days. How did you fare on the test that you crammed for until three o'clock in the morning the night before? Compare that scenario to the instance when you studied ahead of time. Which test did you score better on? The same principle holds true for an IRS examination. One needs to be prepared. Not only will being prepared help you fare much better during an audit, but preparation or planning will save you real dollars on your tax bill.

What are the chances of being audited?

Take the quiz below and test your knowledge of what may or may not increase your chances of being audited:

1. Using an extension of time to file your taxes will increase your chance of being audited.
   a. true
   b. false

2. Reporting a business loss by filing a Schedule C increases the likelihood of an IRS examination.
a. true
b. false

3. Your tax return shows a refund due. The IRS does not usually audit tax returns that show an overpayment in taxes.
a. true
b. false

4. Your occupation alone can increase the possibility of the IRS examining your tax return.
a. true
b. false

5. Using a computer to prepare your taxes will reduce the chance of your tax return being reviewed.
a. true
b. false

6. Amending your taxes is a sure fire way to trigger an audit.
a. true
b. false

7. There are national averages, used by the IRS, as guidelines when assessing acceptable amounts for certain itemized deductions.
a. true
b. false

8. Using the IRS bar codes and peel off labels will increase the likelihood of being auditing.
a. true
b. false

9. The home office deduction is still a red flag today.
a. true
b. false

10. Using whole numbers for deductions on your tax return such as $ 2,000 or $ 5,000 makes it easier for the IRS to process your tax return decreasing your chances of an examination.

a. true

b. false

The answers to the above questions are as follows:

1 (F) 2 (T) 3 (F) 4 (T) 5 (T) 6 (F) 7 (T) 8 (F) 9 (T) 10 (F)

Are you Audit Savvy?

A letter with a return address from the Internal Revenue Service rests in the palm of your hand. Gingerly, you open the envelope to retrieve a single folded piece of paper. The notice begins with the following ominous words "Your Federal Income Tax Return has been selected for examination..." Your day just went to hell in a hand basket. If this scenario became a reality for you, would you be prepared? If you answered no, now is the time for an extreme audit makeover.

1. Be aware of the different degrees of audit intensity.

Correspondence Audit–for minor differences. Usually resolved by correspondence through the mail. Time required – usually minimal. Frequency of this type of audit is greatest.

Office Audit- a formal meeting occurs with an assigned agent at an IRS office. Requires specific documentation to verify the figures reported on your tax return. Time required – usually can be completed in one or two trips. If you are lacking the proper records, time spent can increase substantially.

Field Audit- assigned auditor reviews your records at your location. Time spent at taxpayer's location varies; average time allocated ranges from three days to a week. Review of records is more extensive. Field audits often involve a business.

2. You may be able to call off the audit.

Meet the following three conditions and notify the IRS asking them not to conduct the audit. a) Your tax return was examined for one of the last two years b) There were no changes made by the IRS to the tax return c) The same tax items now cited for examination as those examined previously by the IRS.

3. Put it in writing.

Make sure all correspondence is in writing and sent via certified mail. During the course of either a correspondence, office or field audit, deadlines for responses are assigned. Often, the taxpayer must substantiate that their correspondence was timely remitted. Verbal communications are not evidential.

4. Don't go by yourself.

Take a tax professional with you. This is not the time to frugal with your funds. Would you go to court without an attorney?The old adage that a person who is his own attorney has a fool for a client holds true for those who want to represent themselves in front of the IRS.

5. File an extension of time.

Your current year's tax return, if filed, becomes subject to review. If possible wait until the IRS has concluded its examination before filing the current year's return.

6. You have the right to appeal.

You are unsatisfied with IRS agent's tax examination results. Assert your right to appeal to the agent's supervisor, the Appeals Division of the IRS, and if warranted to the U. S. Tax Court.

Bottom line. Don't feel pressured or rushed to make decisions. Although we all would like to make the experience go away as quickly as possible, don't make a hasty settlement unless you feel it is warranted.

LAST MINUTE TAX MOVES TO MAKE
BEFORE THE END OF THE YEAR!

Here are some tax planning ideas that may save you real dollars when filing your taxes:

1. Consider giving gifts to your children. You may want to shift income since your children are usually in a lower tax bracket. However, bear in mind that if your children are under the age of fourteen, they will be subject to the special "kiddie tax" rates.

2. Don't forget to donate those old clothes that have been stashed away in your closet, by the end of the year. Most importantly, don't forget to get a receipt! Don't overlook unusual donation avenues. Gifting your old computer to your local high school or church and donating your old vehicle to a qualified charity are often missed deductions.

3. Defer income and accelerate deductions. Deferring income into the upcoming year, should result in an overall lower tax bill. You have another year before having to pay tax on these earnings. The trend in Congress has been lowering personal tax rates a little each year. Based on this pattern, accelerate deductions whenever possible. They are worth more today then they will be worth tomorrow.

4. Check the values of your stock holdings. Many taxpayers are carrying into the current year capital losses from previous years. These capital losses can be used to offset capital gains. Selling stocks at a gain and use the capital loss carry forward to offset the gain.

5. If you own a business, the write-off for fixed asset purchases can be accelerated and even can exceed $100,000. 00 in the first year.

6. Don't forget to pay your real estate taxes by December 31st.

7. If you make estimated tax payments to your state, postmark your fourth payment by the December 31st so that it's deductible the current year. Hopefully, you can squeeze a few minutes away from the holiday season to assess whether any of these actions may benefit you.

Congratulations, you've cooked another asset!

Loin of Life Insurance

" Applying for Life Insurance"

Don't buy credit card life insurance that will pay off your outstanding credit card balances in the event of your death. Lets say you have $2,000 balance, you'll probably be charged $13/mth or $156/yr. For about the same amount of money, a 30 yr old female can buy a $100,000 of term life insurance.

This is a truly make ahead recipe. Personally, you will never get the chance to try this recipe but your significant others will be grateful that you have provided this meal for them. You may ask "How will I know it will turn out right?" A make ahead recipe allows you to oversee its creation and if you use the right ingredients

guarantee its success.

Loin of Life Insurance
" Applying for Life Insurance"

Ingredients

The insured (You)

Insurance agent—preferably

Life insurance application

Beneficiary (who you want to give the money to)

$$$ for the premium

Insurance policy

Preparation

1. *Locate an insurance agent that specializes in life insurance.*
2. *Determine what type of life insurance you would like to purchase; term life, whole life or universal life insurance .*
3. *Determine the amount of life insurance coverage you will need.*
1. *Determine who will be the beneficiary (s).*
2. *Complete the life insurance application.*
3. *Pay the requested premium.*
4. *Review the Insurance Policy for accuracy. Generally you have 20 days to cancel the policy and receive a full refund of premium paid.*
5. *On an ongoing basis, reevaluate the amount of coverage you need and the beneficiary (s) you have selected and make any necessary changes.*

Recipe's Financial Nutritional Value
20=Degree of Risk
50=Long Tem Value or Growth Potential
50=Income Producing
15 =Tax Savings

"Sample Section"- Proof of Death Form (Used to file a request for life insurance proceeds.)

COOK YOUR ASSETS LIFE INSURANCE COMPANY

Proof of Death

This form is to be completed upon the death of an insured and forwarded to Cook Your Assets Life Insurance Company. In addition, a certified copy of the official death certificate and the original insurance policy are required. If death was due to suicide, homicide or accidental means, a copy of the investigating officer's report is also required.

> Some companies will only accept a certified death certificate.

STATEMENT OF CLAIM

	Amount of Insurance
ame	
	City, State, Zip
Date of Death	Place of Death
Date of Birth	Place of Birth

Where was date of birth obtained? (Birth or Baptismal Record should be consulted if possible)

When did deceased first complain or give indication of last illness? _____

When did deceased first consult a physician for last illness? _____

Names and addresses of **ALL** physicians who attended or prescribed for deceased within 5 years preceding death:

Physician	Address	Dates of Attendance	Disease or Condition

Names and addresses of **ALL** hospitals where deceased was treated within 5 years preceding death:

Hospital			ase dition

> Some companies will ask for proof of identity ie: drivers license. Others may want the beneficiaries to have their signature notarized.

(Use Separate Sheet If More Space Is Needed)

I certify that the information furnished in support of this claim is true and correct.

WARNING: Any person who knowingly presents a false or fraudulent claim for payment of a loss or benefit or knowingly presents false information in a claim for insurance may be guilty of a crime and subject to fines and confinement in prison.

Date _____ Beneficiary Signature _____ Relationship To Dec____

Beneficiary's Date of Birth _____ Beneficiary's Social Security # _____

Address_____ City, State, Zip _____
        Witness
Date _____ Signature _____ Daytime
                                Telep
Address _____ City, State, Zip _____

> Some companies request the beneficiary to complete a W-9 Form. This is an IRS form that records the beneficiaries social security #.

Authorization to Obtain Information

I hereby authorize any physician or practitioner of the healing arts who has examined or treated the deceased, and all ho_____ ...cilities, insurance companies, health maintenance organizations, Medical Information Bureau, government entity (federal , state _____ ...stitution, or person, that has any information, records or knowledge of him/her or his/her heath, past or present, to furnish suc_____ ...Life Insurance Company or its agents and to permit them to examine and copy such information. I understand that Cook Yo_____ ...has the right to disclose this information to the Medical Information Board, or reinsurers, or agents, employees and others who have a legitimate business interest in obtaining the information in connection with underwriting or claims processing with the company.

Date _____ Signature of Nearest Relative _____ Relationship To Deceased _____

CLW-ULI (12-00)   **Please have Attending Physician complete Page 2.**   Page 1 of 2

WARNING: Any person who knowingly presents a false or fraudulent claim for payment of a loss or benefit or knowingly presents false information in a claim for insurance may be guilty of a crime and subject to fines and confinement in prison.

ATTENDING PHYSICIAN'S STATEMENT

Please answer all questions. This statement is to be furnished without expense to Cook Your Assets Life Insurance Company.

D

| Residence | City, State, Zip |

How long have you known the deceased?

| Date of Death | Place of Death |

If death occurred in a hospital, please give name and address

When were you first consulted for the condition which directly or indirectly caused death?

What was the date of the first symptom or sign according to the clinical history?

How long, in your opinion, did this disease or impairment exist?

Contributory cause of Death

Other Chronic Diseases or Impairments

The attending physician needs to complete this section of the form. Cause of Death is provided with this information.

If death was due to suicide, homicide or accident, please state which _____

Please describe briefly _____

Was an official inquiry held? _____   Was an autopsy made? _____

If so, please give particulars _____

Please give particulars of each condition for which you treated or advised the deceased for the past five years.

Disease	Date	Duration	Result

Please give names and addresses of all other physicians or practitioners who attended deceased within the 5 years preceding death:

Name	Address	City/State	Disease or Impairment

Physician's Signature	Provider Tax ID #		Date
Physician's Name		Degree	
Address		Telephone ( )	
City	State		Zip

Page 2 of 2

"Sample Section"- Proof of Death Form (Used to file a request for life insurance proceeds for an employee under a group life insurance policy.)

COOK YOUR ASSETS LIFE INSURANCE COMPANY

Proof of Death Form

This form is to be completed upon the death of an insured and forwarded to Cook Your Assets Life Insurance Company. In addition, a certified copy of the official death certificate and the original insurance policy are required. If death was due to suicide, homicide or accidental means, a copy of the investigating officer's report is also required.

Certificate/ID Number

Name of Employee	Date of Birth	Date of Death
Address	City, State, Zip	
Date Employed	Date on which employee was last "actively at work"	

Reason Employee stopped work ☐ Death ☐ Disability ☐ Retirement ☐ Termination of Employment

Date on which employment terminated _____

Claim is for (check all applicable)
☐ Basic Group Term Life Amount $ _____ ☐ Accidental Death Amount $ _____
☐ Supplemental/Vol. Group Term Life Amount $ _____ ☐ Optional SeatBelt Rider (if applicable) Amount $ _____

1. Did the deceased die in a motor vehicle accident? ☐ Yes ☐ No   2. Do you recommend payment of this claim? ☐ Yes ☐ No
   If yes, was the deceased wearing a seat belt? ☐ Yes ☐ No

Employer		
Signature	Telephone ( )	
Name (Please print or type)	Title	Date
Address		

Let's hope that your boss likes you!

AUTHORIZATION TO OBTAIN INFORMATION

I hereby authorize any physician or practitioner of the healing arts who has examined or treated the deceased, and all hospitals, clinic or medical related facilities, insurance companies, health maintenance organizations, Medical Information Bureau, government entity (federal, state or local) or other organization, institution, or person, that has any information, records or knowledge of him/her or his/her health, past or present, to furnish such information to Cook Your Assets Life Insurance Company or its agents and to permit them to examine and copy such information. I understand that Cook Your Assets Life Insurance company has the right to disclose this information to the Medical Information Board, or reinsurers, or agents, employees and others who have a legitimate business interest in obtaining the information in connection with underwriting or claims processing with the company.

FRAUD WARNING: Except as noted in separate Fraud Notice, it is or may be a crime to knowingly provide false, incomplete or misleading information to an insurance company for the purposes of defrauding the company or other person. Penalties may include imprisonment, fines, and denial of insurance benefits in accordance with applicable state law.

Date _____ Signature of Nearest Relative _____ Relationship To Deceased _____

BENEFICIARY'S STATEMENT

Beneficiary's Name (Please print) _____ Relationship To Deceased _____

Beneficiary's Date of Birth _____ Beneficiary's Social Security # _____ Daytime Telephone _____

Address _____ City, State, Zip _____

Beneficiary Signature _____

Help! There's so many different types of life insurance! How do I know which one is right for me? And how much do I need?...

You're first question should be "Do I even need life insurance?"

The following are types of people that probably don't need to take out a life insurance policy:

- Children- no one depends on them financially
- Singles- with little debt, with no one depending on them financially and with enough savings to pay for their funeral

- Retired people- with no debt and a tons of savings
- Your pet!

Most people will not fall into these categories and therefore should check out life insurance options.

There are three main types of life insurance coverage:
- Term Life Insurance
- Whole Life Insurance
- Universal Life Insurance

A term life insurance policy provides plain and simple insurance coverage or death benefit.

Whole life and universal life insurance include what is called a cash value- basically some of the money you pay as premium is set aside and eventually given back with some amount of future interest. Yipee for you! Here's another great feature, you can borrow against the money you have paid in, but don't forget you'll be charged interest on your borrowings.

Forgive me. This is my opinion and mine alone. So all you insurance companies out there, please no letters... I just want insurance. Why would I want to mix my insurance needs with my investment needs? This is what whole and universal life policies do. You pay more premium (than term life insurance) and for that extra money, the insurance company invests part of it for you and calls this amount the cash value. This part of your premium is like a forced savings account. Another part of your premium goes to the actual insurance (or the death benefit) and the remaining balance goes to, yes, you guessed it, administrative fees and commissions.

Let's review, whole life and universal insurance policies make you pay more premium to earn a relatively indeterminable amount of interest and pay administrative fees and commissions. Sounds like a great deal to me!

Life insurance is intended to replace your income stream if you die so your dependants will be able to maintain their current standard of living. It is not designed to become your retirement fund. No offense to the insurance industry, but would you want them in charge of your investment activities for the future. In their defense, all the recent unfortunate natural disasters, the insurance industry is barely able to keep its head above water.

So for our discussions, we are going to focus on term life insurance.

We all have responsibilities and obligations to deal with every day. Perhaps you have a mortgage on your house or are paying for your child's college education or are a care provider for your parents.What would happen if you died tomorrow?Would your spouse, children or parents continue to function normally without your financial assistance?

Term life insurance would provide a payout (death benefit) to help pay for these expenses.The first step is to determine how much coverage you will need. The general rule of thumb is to take your annual salary and multiply it by 7. The reality is people buy only as much life insurance that the annual premium that they can afford brings them. Hypothetical example: Martha, a single mom,earns $50,000.00 per year. Using the 7 times earnings rule, she should have a term life insurance policy of $350,000.00. Instead, Martha figures that she can afford an annual premium of $ 400.00. At her age, this premium will buy her a $250,000.00 term life insurance policy. This isn't the right way to choose, but it happens. At least she has some coverage.

I feel a more accurate way to calculate how much insurance you need is to first calculate on an annual basis your living expenses (including mortgage payments and other loans). From this amount deduct any income contributions your dependents make. The resulting amount would then be divided by the current interest rate. Expenses incurred in the future such as educational expenses should be estimated at their annual cost and added to the amount determined for living expenses. Use your best guess of how much these costs will be when determining the annual amount. If interest rates decrease substantially, then you would want to increase your insurance coverage.

Next, you will want to select how long the policy will be in effect. Term insurance policies can be for as short a period as one year or in durations of 5, 10,15,20,25 or 30 years or up to a maximum age.

Renewable and Level are two more terms associated with term insurance policies.

Renewable means that each year, you don't have to pass a physical in order for the policy to stay in effect. The policy automatically renews regardless of your health situation. Unless, the premium difference is very large, I recommend opting for this feature.

Level relates to the premium. Term insurance that does not include this feature would have very low premiums in the beginning of the policy period and very high premiums towards the end of the policy period. Although paying less at first may look attractive, I don't recommend this selection. Later in life when you are in your retirement years, your premium will be very high.

Before we move on to the next recipe, Lemon Pepper Long Term Care Insurance, let's cover a few mistakes people often make when purchasing life insurance.

Purchasing Mortgage Life Insurance - Mortgage Life Insurance is a form of term life insurance by paying off the balance of your mortgage in the event of your death. Here's the negative, as you pay down your mortgage, the face amount of insurance policy also decreases but the premium usually remains the same. Let's see, same premium and less insurance coverage -that doesn't sound good to me.

Also, the insurance proceeds must go to paying off the mortgage and not towards any other expense. So if you had substantial credit card debt that really should be paid off first, here's what would have to happen. The insurance proceeds would have to be used to pay off the mortgage. Then, your heirs would have to refinance your home (hopefully they could qualify for a loan) so that they could get some cash out to pay of the credit card balances. Let's not forget the extra cost incurred for the closing costs for the refinance. Whew! That was busy. I wouldn't bother with the mortgage life insurance; just get term life insurance and be done with it.

Credit Card Life Insurance – I don't recommend buying credit card life insurance that will pay off your outstanding credit card balances in the event of your death. Let's say your average credit card balance is $2,000.00.In order to purchase a $2,000 credit card life insurance policy, you'll probably be charged$ 13/mth or $156/yr. for the premium. Generally, for the same amount of money, a 30 yr old female can buy a $100,000 of term life insurance. Your heirs will have $98,000.00 left over after paying off the credit card balances.

Opting Out of Employer Sponsored Life Insurance. Many

employers offer a certain amount of life insurance as part of their benefits package. Normally the premium pricing is much better than you can get on the outside. Often your employer pays for part of this coverage. There is one potential stumbling block, however. If you leave your job, the cost to convert your group coverage to individual coverage can be shocking. With this in mind, think of your employer's group life insurance policy as a supplemental policy.

Canceling Existing Coverage before Securing New Life Insurance - Try not to test the fate of the gods by having a lapse in coverage. No one plans to have an accident.

Now you're ready to explore your life insurance options!

Congratulations, you've cooked another asset!

Here's a financial diet tip!

Many employers provide their employees with some amount of life insurance. Your employer's policy may not be sufficient for all your life insurance requirements. Often, your company's group policy will only cover your funeral expenses. Also, in most cases, your participation in the group life insurance policy is cancelled if you leave the company. That means, you will be on your own to find alternative coverage.

Lemon Pepper Long Term Care Insurance

" Acquiring Long Term Care Insurance"

> The earlier in life you get a long term care policy, the lower your premiums will be. Don't sign up too early though. The industry is new and undergoing changes. Try to purchase a policy within ten to fifteen years of likely use.

Years ago, families stayed together. Great, great grandparents, grand parents, parents and children all lived under one roof. As members of the family aged, the younger relatives stepped up and took care of their elderly. Many types of animals also herd together in large families taking care of their older members.

Today, the majority of us live apart. One relative is on the west coast while another is on the east coast. We physically can't look after our elderly when we are spattered across the county. Even if we're in the same town, busy schedules and obligations make it difficult to provide the care our aged love ones need. So what is the answer for today's fast paced society? Long term care insurance can provide some piece of mind for all.

Lemon Pepper Long Term Care Insurance

" Acquiring Long Term Care Insurance"

Ingredients

The insured (You) or insurable interest (family member)

Insurance agent

Long term care insurance application

$$$ for the premium

Insurance policy

Preparation

1. Determine your future need for long term care insurance. Will you have enough assets to pay for the potential nursing home costs? Will your family members be financially able to pay for their own nursing costs in the later years. You could obtain insurance for them now instead of having to pay a lot of money later for their care.

2. Find yourself a reputable insurance agent that will help you decide what is the best long term care insurance coverage for you.

3. Complete the insurance application.

4. Pay the specified premium.

5. Review the policy. Most long term care policies have a feature called the "free look" provision. If you find anything in the policy that does not meet your needs, you have 30 days to return the policy and get your money back.

6. On an ongoing basis, reevaluate the amount of coverage you need compared to what you have and make any necessary changes.

Recipe's Financial Nutritional Value
40=Degree of Risk
30=Long Tem Value or Growth Potential
50=Income Producing
60 =Tax Savings

Sample Portion - Long Term Care Questionnaire

Prospect Name: _____
Review Date:_____

THE NEED FOR LONG TERM CARE

Longevity of Life & Gender

The n___ | Its a good idea to review your long term care needs periodically. Your health, finances and personal views may change over time. | *ou get older. If family members haved lived to ___ou will live as long or even longer. The longer ___ding long term care assistance.*

you li___

Statistics say that females live longer. Again the longer you live, the greater your chance of developing a chronic condition that will leave you home bound. Answer these questions to access the past.

To what age did your parents or grandparents live to?

Have many of your family members needed long term care assistance in their later years?

Living Accommodations

For elderly persons living alone, with few friends within close proximity, the potential need for long term care is increased. Do you think your future plans will include or allow for you to live in an assistant living community? If so, part of your "rent" goes for services like daily group meals, bus service etc which would could reduce or delay the need for long term care assistance.

Do you live alone, with a spouse, children or other relatives?

If you have adult children, are they in a position from both location and time to provide you care?

Do you have enough money saved to enable you to stay in an assisted living care community? Some facilities require you to "purchase" an equity interest in the complex, in order to receive all the benefits of their community.

Medical History

Long term care needs usually arise from the result of a chronic disease or ailment. Common suspects are arthritis, heart condition, stroke, emphysema, diabetes, cancer, dementia or Alzheimer's. If any of these conditions are repetitive in your family's history, your risk of experiencing one of these ailments in the future, may be increased. If you currently have a chronic serious health condition, some insurers may not want to insure you. Answer the following question to see what "shape" you are in.

How would you rate your general health? (outstanding, good, fair, poor)

What major surgeries or illnesses have you experienced in the past five years?

What your family's medical history? Are your parents, grandparents still alive?

What medications are you taking and for what reason?

What lifestyle habits or concerns do you have that may lead to future health problems (ie: smoking, overweight, high blood pressure, alcoholism) ?

What may seem harmless today, could cost you in the future. Try to take it easy on those Mango Martinis today so you can be approved for coverage tomorrow.

What would you like?

The questions below are designed to make you assess your future needs. The reality of the future may be scary. Be as honest as possible when responding to these questions, otherwise, you'll only be giving yourself a false sense of security.

Are you absolutely financially secure? Reasonably financially comfortable? Or insecure about your financial condition?

Are you an independant type of person or are you used to leaning on others in times of need?

Will you want your children to have the responsibility of taking care of you later in life?

Will you want to live with your children in their home? Will your children want you to live with them?

If you have no children, who will you rely on to take care of you?

How do you feel about receiving Medicaid assistance?

How would you feel about living in an assisted living community?

Do you want to be able to leave any assets to your family or friends

Are you currently unable to perform daily living without the assista answer yes to this question, you may not be able to purchase long t a temporary condition, get as healthy as possible as soon as possibl

Medicaid covers long term care services if you meet your state's poverty criteria. Generally, "qualifying for poverty" is having $2,000 or less of assets and savings (except for maybe your home and car). Each state's guidelines will vary. You also will be restricted to only those health care providers that accept medicaid patients.

It seems so complicated ... tell me more about long-term care insurance...

Okay, let's start at the beginning by identifying what long-term care covers. The following is a list of services that would fall under long-term care; adult day care, senior centers, skilled nursing care, homemaker/health aides, respite care, medical equipment, certain home repairs and modifications, and hospice care.

Long-term care services can be either skilled nursing care or guardian care to help with the tasks of daily living. These services can be provided in a nursing home, assisted living facility, your home, or an adult day care center. Long-term care is expensive.

Standard insurance does not pay for long-term care. Medicare and medigap cover little long-term care costs. Medicaid will only pay after the patient exhausts their savings.

You could use your savings to pay for these costs. I hesitate to recommend this position. You life savings can be depleted quickly, especially if you need home health services over a prolonged period of time.

Long-term care insurance covers services for people who are unable to care for themselves.

The most common reasons that people need long term insur-ance are:

- A long-drawn-out illness (ie: cancer)
- A cognitive disorder (ie: Alzheimer's)
- A disability
- A degenerative disease (ie: stroke or Parkinson's)

When would benefits be payable?

For most policies, benefits become payable if you need help with two or more of the following activities of daily living (ADL):

- Eating
- Bathing
- Dressing
- Using the toilet
- Maintaining continence
- Cooking

Check your policy to see who determines eligibility. It is better that your own doctor makes the decision rather than the insurance company's representative.

So after reading the above, you're thinking, "I don't want to use my life savings for medical care and I don't want to be a burden to my family, so maybe there's something to this long-term care insurance".

How much coverage, you can afford, depends upon what policy features you choose. Here are some policy features to consider:

Benefit Period: The average nursing home stay is 2 ½ years. Standard benefit periods offered are 2 years through 5 years or for an unlimited period of years. Of course, the longer the period of coverage the higher the cost, so take the longest benefit period you can afford.

Elimination Period: A deductible of sorts. This feature governs how soon the payments begin once you are determined eligible. If you choose, for instance, a thirty day elimination period, you will have to personally pay for your care the first 30 days and your insurance will start paying the 31st day. The longer the elimination period, the lower your premium will be. Estimate how much savings in premium you'll have with a longer elimination period against how much you'll personally have to pay for long term care during the elimination period. This calculation will help you determine what elimination period is best for you based upon your funds available.

Renewal Capability: Virtually all long-term care policies issued today contain a guarantee renewable provision. With this provision, your policy can't be cancelled regardless of your health condition.

Waiver of Premium: This feature allows you to stop paying premiums during the time you are receiving benefits. Check your policy carefully to see if there are any restrictions on this provision, such as you have to be in a nursing home for a certain length of time (usually 90 days) before the premiums are waived.

Inflation Adjustment: This feature increases the benefit amount to cover inflation.

Generally, you can purchase a policy that increases your benefit by 5 % each year. There are three types of inflation adjustments:

Flat benefit- basically there is no increase in the amount of benefit you will receive. The benefit stated on your policy is the benefit you will receive in the future. The premium for this option is the lowest.

Simple interest increases – Each year your original benefit amount is increased by 5%. So if your benefit is $100.00 daily then the following year, your daily benefit amount would increase $5.00. The next year the benefit would again increase $5.00.

Compound Interest increases - the annual benefit increases compound at 5% per year. The same principal, as the simple interest increase, except the second year, would increase by $5.25.This provides the maximum benefit but also carries with it the maximum cost.

Pre-Existing Condition Clause: Most long term policies have a pre-existing condition clause that runs six months from the policy purchase date. Make sure you read the fine print on your policy to see what the duration is.

Alzheimer'sDisease: The trend for most policies is to cover long term care related to Alzheimer's disease. Check your policy though! You want to make sure that this condition is covered. Alzheimer's disease can result in lengthy periods of long term care and high medical costs.

Generally if you've reached your late forties or early fifties, you should be considering whether long- term care insurance will benefit you and your family. Don't wait too much longer after that to make the decision because the premiums will become unreasonable.

Congratulations, you've cooked another asset!

Honey Glazed Home Insurance

" Securing Home Insurance"

> Increasing your deductible can make a big difference in your annual premium– sometimes up to 37%! Ask your agent to quote using different deductibles.

I live in a hurricane prone state. Literally.   In the past few years, I've hosted three hurricanes. I confess, prior to these storms, I never read my homeowner's insurance policy. Today, that's certainly not the case. Not only have I read my policy cover to cover, I've put my insurance company on my phone's speed dial. As with many other recent hurricane victims, my home was totally destroyed. It wasn't until I had to make a claim did I discover how little my insurance policy really covered.

Honey Glazed Home Insurance
" Securing Home Insurance"

Ingredients

Home

Insurance agent

Insurance policy(s)

Pictures of your home

Inventory of your contents

Patience (if you suffer a loss) & perhaps an insurance adjuster

Preparation

1. *Start shopping for an insurance agent prior to your home acquisition. Once you have an idea of what location you want to live in, determine what companies will write insurance in your area. Shop coverage by interviewing several insurance agencies.*

2. *When you've entered into an Offer and Purchase Contract, narrow your insurance search to two or three agents. Your agent will ask questions about the home's structure and the property's exact location. Answering these questions will determine any flood insurance needs and homeowner' insurance rates.*

3. *Request insurance coverage to cover the cost of rebuilding your home at current construction costs. Don't include the cost of your land. Also, don't base replacement cost on the price you paid for the home. If this is a renewal policy, prices most likely have changed since you originally purchased your home.*

4. *Also, request insurance for your contents, additional living expense, liability to others and additional structures.*

5. *Review your policy coverage annually for changes in replacement coverage. Increase coverage for major purchases, renovation and market value increases.*

Recipe's Financial Nutritional Value
30=Degree of Risk
50=Long Tem Value or Growth Potential
20=Income Producing
0=Tax Savings

Sample Homeowners Insurance Quote

COOK YOUR ASSETS INSURANCE COMPANY

Homeowner Quote Summary Sheet

Prepared: 01-27-2008   Quote Number: 5445777

1299
ABC Insurance Agency
123 Main Street
Hometown, USA 99999
1-800-555-3333

Quote Summary

Base Premium	$3,970.00
Additional Premium	$633.00
Total Premium	$4,603.00

Insured	The Financial Chef
Company	Cook Your Assets Insurance Company
Program	Homeowners
State	Florida
Insured Location	123 Main Street
	Hometown, USA 99999
Mailing Address	
Effective Date	02-01-2008
Payment Status	

> If you have a lot of custom work in your house, you may want to ask your agent to increase the amount of coverage on your dwelling. This way you'll be able to replace any damaged property using the same custom work.

Coverage Information

> Hurricane Deductibles are higher then standard policy deductibles. This means you will have to pay more out of pocket before insurance will start reimbursing you for your loss.

Coverage	Limit	Premium
Coverage A: Dwelling	$332,000.00	$3,970.00
Coverage B: Adjacent Structures	$33,200.00	$0.00
Coverage C: Personal Property	$166,000.00	$0.00
Coverage D: Additional Living Expenses	$66,400.00	$0.00
Coverage E: Personal Liability	$300,000.00	$10.00
Coverage F: Medical Payments	$1,000.00	$0.00
Deductible	00.00 AOP / 2% Hurricane	$0.00

The Calendar Year Hurricane Deductible is $6,640.00 (2 % of Coverage A)

> Additional Living Expenses provide you $$$ to live elsewhere if your home is too damaged to live in.

Rating Information

Year Built	1988	Construction	Mason[...]
Territory	USA	Roof	Gable
Protection Class	2	Shutters	None
Building Grade	N	# of Stories	
Residence	Primary	Families	

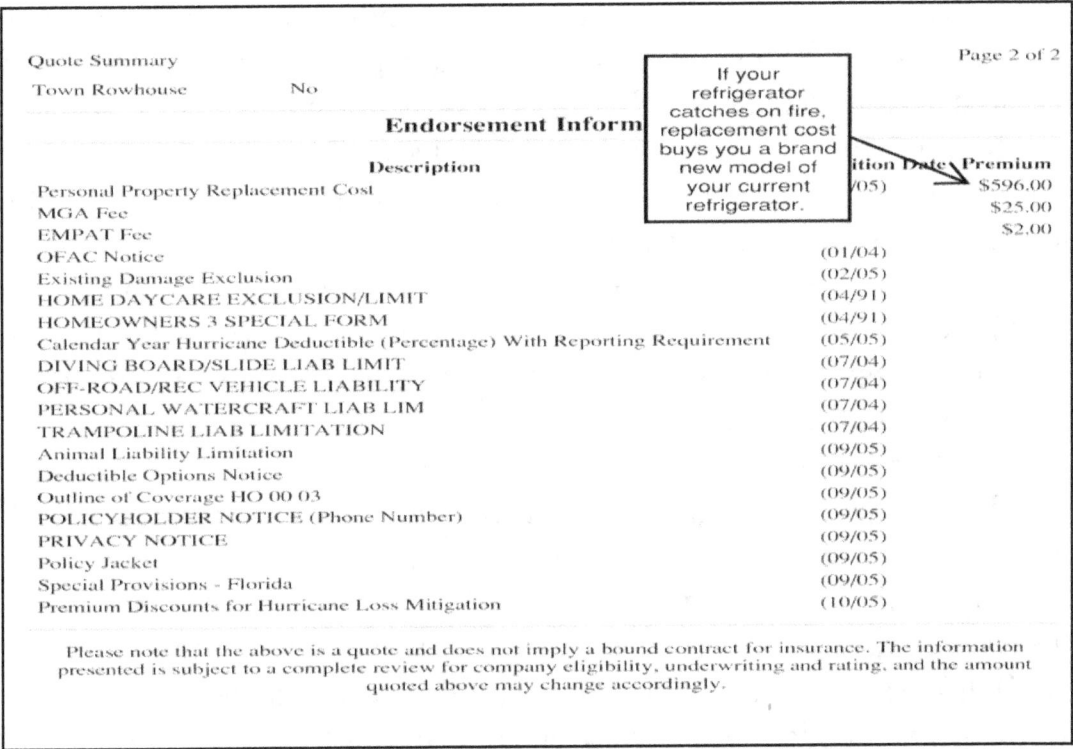

Town Rowhouse   No

Endorsement Inform

Description			Premium
Personal Property Replacement Cost		(05)	$596.00
MGA Fee			$25.00
EMPAT Fee			$2.00
OFAC Notice		(01/04)	
Existing Damage Exclusion		(02/05)	
HOME DAYCARE EXCLUSION/LIMIT		(04/91)	
HOMEOWNERS 3 SPECIAL FORM		(04/91)	
Calendar Year Hurricane Deductible (Percentage) With Reporting Requirement		(05/05)	
DIVING BOARD/SLIDE LIAB LIMIT		(07/04)	
OFF-ROAD/REC VEHICLE LIABILITY		(07/04)	
PERSONAL WATERCRAFT LIAB LIM		(07/04)	
TRAMPOLINE LIAB LIMITATION		(07/04)	
Animal Liability Limitation		(09/05)	
Deductible Options Notice		(09/05)	
Outline of Coverage HO 00 03		(09/05)	
POLICYHOLDER NOTICE (Phone Number)		(09/05)	
PRIVACY NOTICE		(09/05)	
Policy Jacket		(09/05)	
Special Provisions - Florida		(09/05)	
Premium Discounts for Hurricane Loss Mitigation		(10/05)	

Please note that the above is a quote and does not imply a bound contract for insurance. The information presented is subject to a complete review for company eligibility, underwriting and rating, and the amount quoted above may change accordingly.

Still confused? Let's learn more about your insurance options... & let's not forget to cover what to do if you have a claim...

With rising insurance costs, I'm sure there are some of you wondering if you can avoid homeowner's insurance.

The answer is yes. If you own your home mortgage free then there are situations where insurance is not mandatory. If you do so, the reality is you're setting yourself up for a potential catastrophe.

Faulty wiring, leaky pipes, hurricanes- the list goes on and on... all examples of perils that could cause major damage to your home. Insurance coverage would allow you to rebuild without having to spend your own money.

Now, another reality. Most of us are not in the position to pay all cash for our homes. We have mortgages (often massive mortgages), and the bankers that lend us this money will require us to have insurance coverage.

So let's talk deductibles. Your deductible is the amount of money you have to pay towards a loss before your insurance company starts to pay. Your homeowner's policy can have more than one type of deductible.

In the case of a loss by hurricane, you will have to pay the hurricane deductible (usually higher than that of your regular policy). Usually a deductible is a percentage of the policy coverage. For instance, if you have building coverage of $ 100,000.00, your deductible may be 2% of your coverage or $2,000.00. Deductibles also can be expressed as a flat rate, for instance $ 1,000 per occurrence.

Insurance companies are state regulated. Therefore, major changes to items such as premiums, deductibles and coverage require state approval. In Florida, after the hurricanes of 2004, new insurance laws were enacted to help protect the consumer.

I mention this so you are aware to ask your insurance agent of any new laws or pending legislation that may affect your coverage and/or premium. If your agent has no answer, find a new agent.

How much coverage will you need? The amount of homeowner's insurance you need is directly related to the value of your home (not your land). I repeat – Do Not Insure Your Land! You are wasting your money. Homeowner's policies do not cover land. If you live on the beach and half your property is washed away- all I can say is – sorry- your standard policy will not include replacement of your land.

Please realize I'm not saying there isn't one company in the whole world that wouldn't insure you against loss of your "sand". There probably is. But the questions are "At what cost will they insure you and will they ever pay a claim?"

You do want to insure for the following:

Your Dwelling or Building – Coverage A
Your Other Structures- Coverage B
Your Personal Property – Coverage C
Your Loss of Use – Coverage D
Your Liability & Medical– Coverage E & F

You may wonder how other structures differs from your dwelling coverage. Usually, other structures are detached or separate from the main house. Examples are a tool shed in the backyard or a gazebo. Most policies max the amount of coverage for other structures at 10% of the value of your dwelling coverage (Coverage A).

With respect to Coverage A, (your dwelling or building) make sure you obtain replacement coverage and not actual cash value. Replacement coverage will pay you to repair or replace damage at current rates. Still don't understand the difference between replacement coverage versus actual cash value? Here's an example.

You have a ten year old refrigerator. At best it would bring $100 in a garage sale. A fire in your kitchen attacks your refrigerator and leaves it for dead. You file a claim. To replace your refrigerator with a similar brand, your insurance company writes you a check for $1,500.00. You go out and purchase a brand new replacement refrigerator. Had your insurance policy been based upon actual cash value, you would have received less. The replacement price would have been reduced by an amount for depreciation, perhaps resulting in a payment as low as the $100 garage sale price.

Replacement based policies' premiums are slightly higher than actual cash value based policies, but the claims payout normally exceeds the extra premium.

Personal property coverage is usually based upon a percentage of Coverage A- Dwelling. If you have $ 300,000 of Coverage A- your contents coverage will average 50 to 70% of your dwelling coverage or $150,000 to $210,000. TVs, bedroom furniture, lamps, clothes,dishes and silverware are some examples of items that would fall under your contents coverage. Items like your refrigerator, dishwasher, carpeting fall under your building or dwelling coverage.

I can't stress this next point enough. **MAKE SURE YOU HAVE A LIST OF YOUR HOME'S CONTENTS! MAKE SURE YOU HAVE PICTURES OF YOUR HOME'S CONTENTS!** Okay, I've said it; you've been warned.You're thinking what's the big deal? If I have a loss, I'll deal with it then. No, No, No.

Speaking from experience, hurricanes Francis and Jeanne dumped over 4 feet of water into my home. And the water wasn't that pretty natural spring water you drink out of a fancy bottle. No, this water was icky, foul smelling, muddy river water. Piles of river muck and seaweed all flowed to my little abode. Items in my home were unrecognizable. It would have been too late to take pictures or construct an inventory list.

You should make an inventory list and take pictures before you have a loss . Also, update your list for large purchases each year.

If you have an insurance loss, you'll be assigned an adjuster by the insurance company. The adjusters work for the insurance company not for you. They may state that they are paid a commission based upon the total dollar amount of your claim, but bottom line is they work for the insurance company. They will want to see your list and see your pictures.

Some professionals suggest you take a video of your home and your contents. The insurance adjusters I dealt with (and there were many) did not want a video. They had no means to play a video in the field nor did their home office want a video for documentation. They wanted pictures. Pictures became the proof required for you to be reimbursed. To be on the safe side, take pictures and video.

The fourth type of coverage – Loss of Use is a tricky one, at least when it comes to being reimbursed. Loss of use coverage pays you for temporary living arrangements when you're home is uninhabitable. You will most likely face a battle from the insurance company as to whether your home is fit to live in. Fight back! Your insurance company will also be stingy with the length of time they will pay your additional living expenses (ALE). Again, fight back. If you can't get a contractor out to your home for three months, then send your insurance company documentation to support this delay. Settling a claim is a negotiation process to which both you and your insurance company will have to give and take.

The fifth type of coverage- Liability and Medical provide you reimbursement for accidents that happen on your property. Again take pictures of the accident scene, they may be able to help you in your claims settlement.

I want to talk about flood insurance for a moment. Flood insurance is a federally sponsored program. I may get a few politicians angry for stating my opinion, but I feel the national flood insurance program has serious coverage limitations.

Your regular homeowners insurance policy does not cover damage caused by flooding. Instead the federal government has control over flood policies. For residences, the maximum amount of coverage is $250,000.00.Even if your home is worth $500,000.00, the maximum coverage the Federal Flood Insurance Program you can obtain is $250,000.00.

Hurricane Katrina's flood damage was so severe, water levels rose to many of the New Orleans residents' second floors. Damages for many New Orleans homeowners far exceeded the $250,000.00 limit. Homeowners insurance does not want to step up and cover the short fall of flood insurance. In my opinion, this gap is a major defect in the structure of the flood insurance system.

Another major defect in the flood insurance system is that there isn't any coverage for additional living expenses (ALE) (Loss of Use). I found this out the hard way. My home was flooded with river water. Everything was damaged and everything was growing mold. We pulled up carpeting and disposed of furniture and appliances. Salt water destroyed our air handler so we had no air conditioning. The house was not safe. We had to rent an apartment. Our homeowners insurance did have additional living expense but claimed our damage was primarily from flood and tried to deny our ALE claim.

We turned to our Flood Carrier for reimbursement only to find out the Federal Government does not provide for this reimbursement in their flood insurance program. I asked what the rational for this was. One response I received was "Well, the government feels that most homeowners own a two story house so they can just live in the upstairs where there usually isn't any damage. "How absurd is that?Tell that to the survivors of hurricane Katrina where the flood waters were so toxic that their houses were totally contaminated. This flaw is a serious deficiency in the National Flood Insurance Program, in my opinion.

I could provide more examples of how the flood insurance program falls short; instead, I just want to make sure I have gotten the point across that "Flood Insurance is by no means perfect, and you should be aware of the shortcomings relating to the reimbursement for flood claims".

Here are some extra tips with respect to homeowners insurance:

1. STOP SMOKING- some insurers offer to reduce premiums if all residents do not smoke. Smoking accounts for many fire losses each year.
2. COMBINE YOUR AUTO INSURANCE WITH YOUR HOMEOWN-ERS- often insurance companies provide a discount if they have both policies.
3. KEEP THE SAME INSURER- some insurers will give premium reductions for long time policy holders. This discount may become more difficult to achieve as the trend continues for insurance companies to pull out of certain states.

4. TAKE EXTRA STEPS TO MAKE YOUR HOME SAFE- add that smoke detector, burglar alarm, or surveillance camera. Besides providing you extra protection, having these devices may entitle you to receive a credit on your premium.

5. MAKE AN INVENTORY LISTING OF ALL YOUR BELONGINGS AND TAKE PICTURES!! (oh, I think I may have mentioned that already)

Congratulations, you've cooked another asset!

Here's a financial diet tip!

How much should you save?
Factors to consider when determining an amount are: the monthly income you'd like to retire with, your current age, existing credit card debt etc.

Most important is not to set yourself up for failure.
Be realistic. Believing you can save $30,000 a year when your salary is $60,000 is like going on a crash diet. The results for both won't last long.

Financial Chef

Annuities a la Dente

" Purchasing an Annuity"

> Beware! Annuities are not FDIC insured as your bank accounts are. Instead they are guaranteed by life insurance companies. When purchasing an annuity, make sure the life insurance company is very secure and rated high.

An annuity is another way to save money for your retirement years. An annuity has similarities to an IRA account in that the interest and dividends earned are tax free until distributed. Annuities are best for the those with the mind set that they will not touch the money they've set aside for a long while.

Annuities a la Dente
" Purchasing an Annuity"

Ingredients

Person who is licensed to sell insurance

An initial deposit $$$

An annuity application

An annuity agreement

A excellent rated insurance company backing the annuity

In most cases, a beneficiary

Preparation

1. First decide how much you have in available funds. Is it a one time deposit? Or can you make more payments into the future?
2. Find a good financial advisor or insurance agent licensed to sell annuities. This person can work for a bank, brokerage firm, financial planning company or be an independent financial advisor.
3. Complete the annuity application.
4. Decide if you want a deferred or immediate annuity. If you choose a deferred annuity, decide if you want a fixed or variable annuity.
5. Verify what is the minimum interest rate the annuity will pay. Usually annuities offer a higher initial interest rate to get you interested. Often, this rate only lasts for a year.
6. Ask about the surrender charges and the agent's commissions.
7. Review the Annuity Agreement

Recipe's Financial Nutritional Value
40=Degree of Risk
50=Long Tem Value or Growth Potential
25=Income Producing
20 =Tax Savings

Sample Portion of Annuity Application

Annuity Application To Cook Your Assets
Underwriters Life Insurance Co.

1. PROPOSED ANNUITANT_____ SOC. SECURITY NO._____

2. DATE OF BIRTH_____ PLACE OF BIRTH_____ SEX_____

3. OWNER'S MAILING ADDRESS (include Zip or Postal Code and any apt. no.)_____
_____

4. ANNUITY PLAN ELECTED: ☐ Flexible Premium ☐ single Premium Deferred

> If you choose tax qualified, you must choose to the right a box of what type of plan it is. The contributions to a tax qualified plan are tax deductible.

5. ☐ TAX QUALIFIED PLAN (check one) ☐ IRA ☐ SEP ☐ PT ☐ KEOGH
   ☐ NON-TAX QUALIFIED PLAN ☐ Limited Joint Control
   ☐ Other_____

> With Tax Qualified Plans, the premiums are tax deductible while with Non-Tax Qualified Plans, the premiums are not tax deductible.

6. MATURITY DATE_____

7. ☐ DEPOSIT (premium) AMOUNT $_____
   ☐ BASE DEPOSIT (premium) on Immediate Annuity with Payments of $_____ each. payable
   ☐ Annually ☐ Semi-annually ☐ Quarterly ☐ Monthly Payments to begin _____
                                                                      Month Day Year

8. DEPOSIT (Premium) MODE: ☐ Single Premium ☐ Annual ☐ Semi-Annual ☐ Quarterly
   ☐ Monthly ☐ Monthly Bank Draft ☐ Government Allotment
   CASH PAID With/APPLICATION $_____ (If none, enter "NONE.")

> Timing of when you pay your premiums is flexible.

9. BILL TO: ☐ Annuitant ☐ Other (print name)

10. POLICY DATE: ☐ DATE OF ISSUE OR ☐ OTHER_____

11. Is this annuity intended:
    (a) to replace, in whole or in part, any existing insurance or annuity? ☐ Yes ☐ No
    (b) to be purchased from other insurance or annuity proceeds? ☐ Yes ☐ No
    If yes, to (a) or (b), give company name, policy number, amount (of coverage) and plan for each policy.
    _____
    _____

Annuity(3-90)   IAP1-2

12. JOINT ANNUITANT: (full name, mailing address, and relationship to Proposed Annuitant)_____

_____

13. BENEFICIARY (Subject to change. Full Name, Address, Phone, and Relationship)

_____
_____
_____
_____
_____
_____

14. ADDITIONAL OTHER, DETAILS, AND SPECIAL REQUESTS (Indicate Question Number)

_____
_____
_____
_____

THOSE WHO SIGN THIS APPLICATION AGREE THAT:

1. All of the statements in this application are correctly recorded, and are complete and true to the best of the knowledge and belief of those who made them.

2. No Agent is authorized to accept risks, make or change contracts, or give up any of the Insurer's rights or requirements.

3. Unless otherwise stated in question 14, the Applicant will own the policy and the Proposed Annuitant (if not Applicant) will be the successor owner.

4. To put the policy issued in force, the policy must be delivered to applicant.

Dated at_____ on _____ day of _____, 20____

Signature of Proposed Annuitant (applicant),_____

Signature of Applicant (if not Proposed Annuitant),_____

(PRINT Applicant's Name, Address, Relationship to Proposed Annuitant, Social Security Number)

I represent that: 1) I am a duly licensed agent of this insurance company; 2) I have truly and accurately recorded all answers given to me; 3) I have explained the provisions of the policy being applied for; and 4) if a deposit has been rendered, I have given a company receipt for initial premium in the amount of $_____ which as been paid to me by:　[ ] check　[ ] cash　[ ] money order.

Witness_____
　　　　　　　　　　　Agent　　　　　　　　　　　　　　　　　Date

_____
Countersigned by licensed resident agent (if required)

ANNUITANT_____

Annuity(3-90)　　　　　　　　　　　　　　　　　　　　　　　　　　IAP1-2

Nice to see the agent taking some liability!

Still not clear what an annuity is? Read on...

An annuity is an investment secured by the financial strength of an insurance company. Wow, that's pretty scary to me, but I live in Florida. It's hard enough to find an insurance company to write a policy here, let alone find one that is financially strong. I can say this because my insurance carrier just declared insolvency and has been taken over by the State of Florida.

If the financial professional that's selling you the annuity doesn't provide you documentation of the insurance company's rating, it's time to find another agent.

First, let's discuss the types of annuities, and then let's explore who may benefit from investing in an annuity.

There are three basic types of annuities:

- Fixed
- Variable
- Equity-Indexed

Each of these annuity types has an accumulation phase and a paying out phase. The accumulation phase is just as it sounds. You make either a single payment or a series of payments. The premium(s) you pay earn income and accumulates in your account. This is the accumulation phase. The additional earnings are tax -free until you get to (okay, you guessed it) the paying out phase.

This phase is the period or periods during which you will be paid back. A deferred annuity means the investor will receive payment(s) at some later date. An immediate payout means the investor will begin receiving payments right after the purchase date.

Restating, all three types of annuities have an accumulation phase and paying out phase. Let's now look at how these annuities differ.

Fixed Annuities

In this case, you give a sum of money to an insurance company, and in exchange they promise to give you a fixed monthly amount for a certain period of time. The monthly amount can either be for a fixed period of time (ie: 20 years) or can continue until your death.

If you choose a lifetime payment arrangement, think about this. Bluntly stated, what if you die and you've only received two months payments?Your investment now belongs to the insurance company. Okay, I know there are some of you asking, "Well, what if you live to be 100?" Sounds like gambling, but without the fun. Some fixed annuities allow you to have a lifetime payment arrangement for both you and then for your beneficiary's lifetime. This will reduce the risk, but you'll pay more for that safety.

Fixed annuities allow you to lock in a guaranteed rate of return for periods ranging from one year to ten years. Rates may fluctuate, but they will never drop below the guaranteed rate. Make sure you know the guaranteed rate as well as the current rate quoted for the annuity. The guaranteed rate is always lower than the market rate when an agent is showing you the annuity's attributes. The current rate may look attractive, but it's not a sure thing. Ask yourself if you would be happy with earning at the guaranteed rate? If not, you should move on.

Equity-Indexed Annuities

Equity-indexed annuities are like a fixed annuity. You get a guaranteed rate and fixed payments with this investment. However, the equity-indexed provides for more growth potential because it's tied to an index such as the Standard and Poor's 500. Okay, hang with me for just a moment more; I know this is getting a little technical. The Standard and Poor's 500 Index basically tracks the performance of 500 large-cap (really big) publicly traded companies. So if the big guys do well then your annuity does well. There is some risk owning an equity-indexed annuity, but not as much as a variable annuity.

Variable Annuities

A variable annuity is more complex and risky. For that extra risk you have the possibility to earn a better rate of return. Possibility. Not guaranteed.

With a variable annuity, money is invested in accounts similar to mutual funds. Just like mutual funds, your account can see great gains or experience some real losers. Variable annuities are not for the faint at heart. There are more fees associated with variable annuities. Mortality fees, administrative, and record maintenance charges are assessed.

Perhaps the most negative facets of annuities are the surrender charges. If you withdraw money from your account prior to a certain time period, a surrender charge is assessed. Usually this charge is a percentage of the amount withdrawn. Why are surrender charges assessed? Fees are needed to be collected to cover the initial expenses of selling you the annuity contract. Yes, the majority of the surrender charge is used to cover the high-commission agents receive when they sell you the investment, especially variable annuity policies.

So unless you can hang in there for the long term, annuities may not be right for you.

Who is a model annuity buyer? An individual who fits the following criteria:

- They are concerned that they will outlive their savings.
- They are making the maximum contributions to their IRAs and other retirement plans.
- They can live without the money until after the age of 59 ½.

Speaking frankly, how many of us meet the last two criteria?

Congratulations, you've cooked another asset!

Section V

Desserts for the
Golden Years

❧ ❧

Okay, so a recipe for preparing your last will and testament may not be your choice for dessert. And you can't skip these recipes because you're on a diet. You need these recipes for your peace of mind. These recipes will comfort those close to you and help them make decisions in difficult times. What type of funeral do you want? Do you want to be put on life sustaining machines? These are questions that you should not leave unanswered. If these decisions are hard for you, can you imagine how difficult they are for your loved ones?

Keep in mind that you can always change some of the ingredients used in dessert recipes. Today, you are totally in love with your boyfriend, Jimmy. Next month, Jimmy runs off with the Starbuck's counter girl. Still want to leave him your nest egg? You need to continuously review dessert recipes to determine if the ingredients need to be adjusted.

So make these recipes ahead of time, and your family will be thankful to you for doing so.

Here's a financial diet tip!

Try making an extra mortgage payment each year. Making extra payments will cut down on the length of your mortgage and the amount of interest you pay over the life of the loan. The specifics depend on the size of your loan and your interest rate. Even if it's an extra $100.00 towards the principal balance each month, the savings will add up!

Financial Chef

Strawberry Shortcake Social Security Benefits

"Applying for Social Security Benefits"

Under certain conditions, did you know that you may be able to recover social security benefits on your ex-husband or ex-wife? At least, they may be good for something!

"Wow! You mean when I get old the government is going to pay me money? That's hot!" If that's what you're thinking– stop. Many widely respected economic forecasters question the reliability of the social security system. Even if the money is there when you get old, its not that great a deal. You pay to the government social security taxes all your working life. When you get old, you get the money back. Your taxed when you earn it and unfortunately for many, your taxed when you take it.

Strawberry Shortcake Social Security Benefits

"Applying for Social Security Benefits"

Ingredients

Internet connection or telephone

Your social security number

Your birth certificate

Latest W-2 forms or personal tax return

Proof of citizenship, if you were not born in the U.S.

Preparation

1. First decide if you want to start receiving benefits early (starting with age 62).

2. Apply three months prior to when you want benefits to begin.

3. Either go to a social security office in your area or go online to www.socialsecurity.gov or 1-800 772-1213. A representative will make an appointment for your application.

4. Provide the necessary documentation for proof of identity to the Social Security Office ie: birth certificate, W-2s etc.

5. Provide the bank account information to the representative for direct deposit.

6. Check your bank statement to verify your deposits are being made.

7. An ongoing basis, inform the social security of address changes, income changes and name changes

8. Enjoy your retirement!

Recipe's Financial Nutritional Value
10=Degree of Risk
50=Long Tem Value or Growth Potential
30=Income Producing
10=Tax Savings

Sample Section of Social Security Statement For Illustrative Purposes

Prevent identity theft—protect your Social Security number

Your Social Security Statement

Prepared especially for Wanda Worker

January 24, 2007

See inside for your personal information →

www.socialsecurity.gov

WANDA WORKER
456 ANYWHERE AVENUE
MAINTOWN, USA 11111-1111

Section of "Social Security Statement" presented for illustrative purposes only.

What's inside...

What Social Security Means To You

This *Social Security Statement* will help you understand what Social Security means to you and your family. This *Statement* can help you better plan for your financial future. It gives you estimates of your Social Security benefits under current law. Each year, we will send you an updated *Statement* including your latest reported earnings.

Be sure to read this *Statement* carefully. If you think there may be a mistake, please let us know. That's important because your benefits will be based on our record of your lifetime earnings. We recommend you keep a copy of this *Statement* with your financial records.

Social Security is for people of all ages...
It can help you whether you're young or old, male or female, single or with a family. It's there for you when you retire, but it's more than a retirement program. Social Security also can provide benefits if you become disabled and help support your family when you die.

Work to build a secure future...
Social Security is the largest source of income for most elderly Americans today. It is very important to remember that Social Security was never intended to be your only source of income when you retire. Social Security can't do it all. You also will need other savings, investments, pensions or retirement accounts to make sure you have enough money to live comfortably when you retire.

About Social Security's future...
Social Security is a compact between generations. For more than 70 years, America has kept the promise of security for its workers and their families. But now, the Social Security system is facing serious future financial problems, and action is needed soon to make sure that the system is sound when today's younger workers are ready for retirement.

Today there are more than 37 million Americans age 65 or older. Their Social Security retirement benefits are funded by today's workers and their employers who jointly pay Social Security taxes — just as the money they paid into Social Security was used to pay benefits to those who retired before them. Unless action is taken soon to strengthen Social Security, in just 10 years we will begin paying more in benefits than we collect in taxes. Without changes, by 2040 the Social Security Trust Fund will be exhausted.* By then, the number of Americans 65 or older is expected to have doubled. There won't be enough younger people working to pay all of the benefits owed to those who are retiring. At that point, there will be enough money to pay only about 74 cents for each dollar of scheduled benefits. We will need to resolve these issues soon to make sure Social Security continues to provide a foundation of protection for future generations as it has done in the past.

Social Security on the Net...
Visit *www.socialsecurity.gov* on the Internet to learn more about Social Security. You can read our publications, use the *Social Security Benefit Calculators* to calculate future benefits, apply for retirement, spouse's or disability benefits, or subscribe to *eNews* for up-to-date information about Social Security.

Linda S. McMahon
Acting Commissioner of Social Security

* These estimates of the future financial status of the Social Security program were produced by the actuaries at the Social Security Administration based on the intermediate assumptions from the Social Security Trustees' Annual Report to the Congress.

Your Estimated Benefits

*Retirement You have earned enough credits to qualify for benefits. At your current earnings rate, if you
stop working and start receiving benefits...
At age 62, your payment would be about... .... $ 975 a month
If you continue working until...
your full retirement age (67 years), your p... $ 1,412 a month
age 70, your payment would be about .... $ 1,761 a month

> The longer you wait
> to start taking your
> benefits the larger your
> check will be.

^Disability You have earned enough credits to qualif.. right now,
your payment would be about .... $ 1,293 a month

*Family If you get retirement or disability benefits, your spouse and children also may qualify for benefits.

*Survivors You have earned enough credits for your family to receive survivors benefits. If you die this
year, certain members of your family **may** qualify for the following benefits:
Your child .... $ 1,008 a month
Your spouse who is caring for your child .... $ 1,008 a month
Your spouse, if benefits start at full retirement age... $ 1,344 a month
Total family benefits cannot be more than... $ 2,473 a month
Your spouse or minor child may be eligible for a special one-time death benefit of $255.

Medicare You have enough credits to qualify for Me... etire at age 65, be sure
to contact Social Security three months be.................................. Medicare.

> Your spouse and your
> children may be eligible
> to receive benefits, if
> you have passed away.

 * **Your estimated benefits are based on** .... hanges to the law in the
 past and can do so at any time. The la .... change because, by 2040,
 the payroll taxes collected will be eno .... of scheduled benefits.

We based your benefit estimates on these facts:
Your date of birth ....April 5, 1966
Your estimated taxable earnings per year after 2006 ....$38,626
Your Social Security number (only the last four digits are shown to help prevent identity theft)............XXX-XX-1234

How Your Benefits Are Estimated

To qualify for benefits, you earn "credits" through your work — up to four each year. This year, for example, you earn one credit for each $1,000 of wages or self-employment income. When you've earned $4,000, you've earned your four credits for the year. Most people need 40 credits, earned over their working lifetime, to receive retirement benefits. For disability and survivors benefits, young people need fewer credits to be eligible.

We checked your records to see whether you have earned enough credits to qualify for benefits. If you haven't earned enough yet to qualify for any type of benefit, we can't give you a benefit estimate now. If you continue to work, we'll give you an estimate when you do qualify.

What we assumed — If you have enough work credits, we estimated your benefit amounts using your average earnings over your working lifetime. For 2007 and later (up to retirement age), we assumed you'll continue to work and make about the same as you did in 2005 or 2006. We also included credits we assumed you earned last year and this year.

Generally, estimates for older workers are more accurate than those for younger workers because they're based on a longer earnings history with fewer uncertainties such as earnings fluctuations and future law changes.

These estimates are in today's dollars. After you start receiving benefits, they will be adjusted for cost-of-living increases.

We can't provide your actual benefit amount until you apply for benefits. **And that amount may differ from the estimates stated above because:**
(1) Your earnings may increase or decrease in the future.
(2) Your estimated benefits are based on current law.
 The law governing benefit amounts may change.

(3) Your benefit amount may be affected by **military service, railroad employment or pensions earned through work on which you did not pay Social Security tax.** Following are two specific instances. You can also visit *www.socialsecurity.gov/mystatement* to see whether your Social Security benefit amount will be affected.

Windfall Elimination Provision (WEP) — In the future, if you receive a pension from employment in which you do not pay Social Security taxes, such as some federal, state or local government work, some nonprofit organizations or foreign employment, and you also qualify for your own Social Security retirement or disability benefit, your Social Security benefit may be reduced, but not eliminated, by WEP. The amount of the reduction, if any, depends on your earnings and number of years in jobs in which you paid Social Security taxes, and the year you are age 62 or become disabled. For more information, please see *Windfall Elimination Provision* (Publication No. 05-10045) at *www.socialsecurity.gov/WEP*.

Government Pension Offset (GPO) — If you receive a pension based on federal, state or local government work in which you did not pay Social Security taxes and you qualify, now or in the future, for Social Security benefits as a current or former spouse, widow or widower, you are likely to be affected by GPO. If GPO applies, your Social Security benefit will be reduced by an amount equal to two-thirds of your government pension, and could be reduced to zero. Even if your benefit is reduced to zero, you will be eligible for Medicare at age 65 on your spouse's record. To learn more, please see *Government Pension Offset* (Publication No. 05-10007) at *www.socialsecurity.gov/GPO*.

Your Earnings Record

Years You Worked	Your Taxed Social Security Earnings	Your Taxed Medicare Earnings
1982	550	550
1983	1,299	1,299
1984	2,254	2,254
1985	3,704	3,704
1986	4,962	4,962
1987	6,282	6,282
1988	7,827	7,827
1989	10,041	10,041
1990	12,297	12,297
1991	14,278	14,278
1992	16,399	16,399
1993	17,772	17,772
1994	19,346	19,346
1995	21,057	21,057
1996	22,946	22,946
1997	25,031	25,031
1998	26,991	26,991
1999	29,072	29,072
2000	31,251	31,251
2001	32,542	32,542
2002	33,380	33,380
2003	34,720	34,720
2004	36,756	36,756
2005	38,626	38,626
2006	Not yet recorded	Not yet recorded

Did you know... Social Security is more than just a retirement program? It's here to help you when you need it most.

You and your family may be eligible for valuable benefits:

When you die, your family may be eligible to receive survivors benefits.

Social Security may help you if you become disabled—even at a young age.

It is possible for a young person who has worked and paid Social Security taxes in as few as two years to become eligible for disability benefits.

Social Security credits you earn move with you from job to job throughout your career.

Check your records and make sure that your earnings are presently correctly. If not, contact the social security administration to make sure they update your records.

Total Social Security and Medicare taxes paid over your working career throug

Estimated taxes paid for Social Security:		Estimated taxes paid for Medicare:	
You paid:	$27,730	You paid:	$6,506
Your employers paid:	$27,730	Your employers paid:	$6,506

Note: You currently pay 6.2 percent of your salary, up to $97,500, in Social Security taxes and 1.45 percent in Medicare taxes on your entire salary. Your employer also pays 6.2 percent in Social Security taxes and 1.45 percent in Medicare taxes for you. If you are self-employed, you pay the combined employee and employer amount of 12.4 percent in Social Security taxes and 2.9 percent in Medicare taxes on your net earnings.

Help Us Keep Your Earnings Record Accurate

You, your employer and Social Security share responsibility for the accuracy of your earnings record. Since you began working, we recorded your reported earnings under your name and Social Security number. We have updated your record each time your employer (or you, if you're self-employed) reported your earnings.

Remember, it's your earnings, not the amount of taxes you paid or the number of credits you've earned, that determine your benefit amount. When we figure that amount, we base it on your average earnings over your lifetime. If our records are wrong, you may not receive all the benefits to which you're entitled.

Review this chart carefully using your own records to make sure our information is correct and that we've recorded each year you worked. You're the only person who can look at the earnings chart and know whether it is complete and correct.

Some or all of your earnings from **last year** may not be shown on your *Statement*. It could be that we still

were processing last year's earnings reports when your *Statement* was prepared. Your complete earnings for last year will be shown on next year's *Statement*. **Note:** If you worked for more than one employer during any year, or if you had both earnings and self-employment income, we combined your earnings for the year.

There's a limit on the amount of earnings on which you pay Social Security taxes each year. The limit increases yearly. Earnings above the limit will not appear on your earnings chart as Social Security earnings. (For Medicare taxes, the maximum earnings amount began rising in 1991. Since 1994, **all** of your earnings are taxed for Medicare.)

Call us right away at **1-800-772-1213** (7 a.m.–7 p.m. your local time) if any earnings for years **before last year** are shown incorrectly. If possible, have your W-2 or tax return for those years available. (If you live outside the U.S., follow the directions at the bottom of page 4.)

When can I start collecting benefits? Can I keep working? Tell me more...

Applying for Social Security benefits is a fairly straight-forward process. Most of the application process can be completed online. After you start receiving benefits, you will be responsible for reporting certain changes.

Here are some of the changes that you will need to report to the administration:

- ➢ Move (change of address)
- ➢ Estimated earnings change
- ➢ Change of your direct deposit banking account
- ➢ Marriage or divorce
- ➢ Change of name
- ➢ Citizenship changes

Most of the above changes are self- explanatory.

However, the line item "estimated earnings change" may be unclear.

First, you can work while you are eligible to receive social security benefits. This news is probably not what you want to hear. Who wants to still be working when you can hardly get out of bed in the morning? It gets even better. So, now you're working when many of your body parts aren't anymore. At age 63, you get your realtor's license. You sell a two million dollar home. You get a big fat commission check. You buy lunch for everyone in the office. You take your husband out for a fancy dinner. Stop! You better save some of that windfall because if you earn too much income, your Social Security benefits will be reduced.

If you have not yet reached full retirement age but are receiving benefits, there is a limit to the amount of earned income you can make. Generally, if you go over the limit, your benefits will be reduced $1 for every $2 of excess earnings.

In the year that you reach full retirement age, if you exceed the limit of earned income, the reduction of benefits is $1 for every $3 of excess earnings.

What counts as earned income? Wages, vacation pay, sick pay and net self-employment income are earned income. Dividends, interest income, capital gains, pensions are not earned income.

What if you don't report an increase in earnings? The Social Security administration will catch up to you and request you to return the overpayment. Ugh! Personally, I'd rather not have the money at all, if I know I'll have to repay it.

Will the increase in my earnings also increase my future benefits? The answer is no. Every October, Social Security recalculates your benefits based upon earnings from the prior year and back. Unless your last year's wages turn out to be one of your highest earning years, your benefit won't increase. Chances are earned income in your retirement years is less than when you were younger.

Once you reach full retirement age, you may keep all your retirement benefits, no matter how much money you earn.

The simple illustration above is used to make you aware that when you are close to retirement be careful of the amount of income you earn. You may have to pay back some of the Social Security benefits you received depending on the amount you earn and you age when you earn it. The Social Security administration continuously changes the earning limits and the age you need to attain for full retirement. The current trend is for the government to keep raising the full retirement age. When your time is approaching, contact the Social Security administration office in your neighborhood and get the current facts.

As of the writing of this book, you can retire any time between 62 and full retirement age. If you retire prior to full retirement you will have a smaller monthly check than if you wait until full retirement age. The reduction in the benefit amount is permanent. The trade off is earlier benefits for a smaller amount.

There is a "break even age," which is the age that you would have to reach before the delayed higher retirement benefits would exceed the earlier lower retirement benefits. There is an online calculator on the Social Security website or you can call an administrator who will calculate this age for you.

Okay, all you divorced people out there! Guess what? You may be eligible to receive Social Security benefits based on the earnings of the ex! Yippee! There are some restrictions that must be met, so let's see if you'll qualify. First, you must have been married for ten years. You also must be divorced for at least two years. You can't remarry while your former husband is alive. You need the ex's social security number and their whereabouts.

Isn't this great? Here are some other tidbits of information on the issue.

- ➢ You would receive the spousal portion (50%) of the ex's benefits when you reach both 62.
- ➢ You can collect, whether or not your ex is collecting. The ex only has to be eligible to collect for you to receive benefits.
- ➢ Even if your ex remarries, you still collect. For those ridiculously compassionate divorcees, you'll be comforted to know that the new wife also can collect on your worthless ex-spouse.
- ➢ If you ex dies, your portion increases to 100% of their benefit. Please don't get any ideas out there!
- ➢ Don't worry if none of the divorce documents you signed state that you are entitled to these benefits. This is federal law.

Anther recipe you can make that has the same basic ingredients as Strawberry Shortcake Social Security Benefits, is Mocha Mud Pie Medicare. You will want to make this recipe when you reach age 65. Use all the same ingredients as the Strawberry Shortcake recipe only omitting the latest W-2 Form or personal tax return.

Ask an average U. S. citizen the following question. "Name a U. S. government program that needs a facelift? " Popular answer is Social Security and Medicare. Common belief is that these two programs act as one. My belief is that you can't rely solely on either to provide for your retirement needs.

If Social Security benefits will be your only source of retirement income, you may find yourself really struggling financially in the later years. If Medicare will be your only source of medical insurance, again, you may find yourself financially strapped.

I have seen many situations where an elderly person recovers from an operation physically but not mentally because they believed Medicare would pay for all their doctor bills. Medicare insurance charges deductibles and co-pays to the patient that can often add up to big debt.

There are four parts to Medicare:

Medicare Part A- Hospital Insurance- services primarily for inpatient hospital care (surgeries etc), skilled nursing, and hospice care.

Medicare Part B- Medical Insurance- services for doctors fees, outpatient hospital visits, labs etc. You pay a monthly premium for this coverage.

Medicare Part C- also called Medicare Advantage – acts like a PPO or HMO and may lower your costs of medical service and provide extra benefits for an additional monthly fee. You must elect to have this coverage. Medicare Advantage acts in some ways as secondary insurance.

Medicare Part D- provides prescription drug coverage. You must elect to have this fairly new coverage.

Medicare Parts A & B do not cover hospital deductibles and Medicare Part B co-pays. Medicare also deems certain medical procedures unnecessary and will refuse to pay a claim for these services. What Medicare may consider unnecessary, you may find essential. But can you afford to pay for the procedure out of pocket? Secondary insurance and Medigap provide additional health insurance protection in an attempt to cover these items Medicare doesn't provide for.

You are responsible for 20% of the charges resulting from Medicare Part B services. It doesn't take long for these charges to start to add up to real dollars.

Here's the scary part. In the future, these two recipes may become extinct. Will you be ready with substitutes for these staples? Your lifetime menu may depend on it. Everyone should consider this possibility and have a back up plan in mind. Hopefully, you can replace these recipes with tastier alternatives that are less costly to prepare.

Congratulations, you've cooked another asset!

Here's a financial diet tip!

Sometimes realizing when to shop can result in great bargains. Certain months are know for their sales. January is famous for linen sales. The month of August is great for special deals on outdoor furniture and summer clothes. Also, make sure to check out car and computer close-out sales in December! Some deals just shouldn't be passed up!

Financial Chef

Lemon Meringue Living Wills

"Executing a Living Will"

> Stopping artificial life support is a hard decision to make. If its tough for you to make up your mind, imagine how difficult it would be for a family member to have to make that decision for you.

Many people confuse a living will with a last will and testament.

A living will is a document outlining your particular wishes for when you are still alive. It specifically addresses that you do not want artificial life support should you become terminally ill or enter into a irreversible coma. A last will and testament is a document outlining who receives your property and who will manage the your estate upon your death. Each document tries to clearly express your intentions and reduce any family misunderstandings.

Lemon Meringue Living Will

"Executing a Living Will"

Ingredients

Ability to make some tough decisions

Attorney

Two independent witnesses

A notary public

A physician (optional)

Preparation

1. *Make some hard decisions about whether you would want to be kept alive on life support.*
2. *Retain an attorney to prepare the document. The law varies from state to state. This is an important document. Do not try to do this on-line.*
3. *Review the document.*
4. *Sign and notarize the document in front of two independent witness.*
5. *Distribute copies of the living will to your physician and significant others.*
6. *If you move to another state, check the law to see if your living will is valid in your new residence.*

Recipe's Financial Nutritional Value
0=Degree of Risk
10=Long Tem Value or Growth Potential
10=Income Producing
0=Tax Savings

Sample Living Will Document

Living Will Declaration
For
The Financial Chef

Copies of your living will should be given to your physician, spouse or a key family member, and your named health care surrogate.

This declaration is made this _____ day of_____

I, _____, being of sound mind, willfully and voluntarily make known my desires that my moment of death shall not be artificially postponed.

If at any time I should have an incurable and irreversible injury, disease, or illness judged to be a terminal condition by my attending physician who has personally examined me and has determined that my death is imminent except for death delaying procedures, I direct that such procedures which would only prolong the dying process be withheld or withdrawn, and that I be permitted to die naturally with only the administration of medication, sustenance, or the performance of any medical procedure deemed necessary by my attending physician to provide me with comfort care.

In the absence of my ability to give directions regarding the use of such death delaying procedures, it is my intention that this declaration shall be honored by my family and physician as the final expression of my legal right to refuse medical or surgical treatment and accept the consequences from such refusal.

Signed _____

City, County and State of Residence _____

Although this form does not include a spot for a notarized signature, it is advisable for a living will to be notarized.

The declarant is personally known to me and I believe him or her to be of sound mind. I saw the declarant sign the declaration in my presence (or the declarant acknowledged in my presence that he or she had signed the declaration) and I signed the declaration as a witness in the presence of the declarant. I did not sign the declarant's signature above for or at the direction of the declarant. At the date of this instrument, I am not entitled to any portion of the estate of the declarant according to the laws of intestate succession or, to the best of my knowledge and belief, under any will of declarant or other instrument taking effect at declarant's death, or directly financially responsible for declarant's medical care.

Witness _____

Witness _____

Two witness signatures are required in order for a living will to be valid.

Ask more questions about a living will...

What is a living will?

A living will is a document outlining certain health care related issues that apply while you are still alive. A living will becomes effective when you are not able to make decisions about your health. It simply states that you do not want artificial life support if you become either terminally ill or lapse into an irreversible coma or vegetative state.

Do laws change from state to state for living wills?

Yes. That's why I suggest you retain an attorney familiar with your state's rules. Also, if you moved to another state and already have a living will in place, check to be sure it is still valid.

What is a Surrogate Health Care Designation?

It is a person whom you name as your representative to make medical decisions for you if you are unable to make them yourself. A legal document which appoints a health care surrogate is called a Health Care Power of Attorney.

A health care surrogate can't override a living will's instructions.

What conditions does my living will address?

- That you do not want your doctor to use extraordinary means or artificial nutrition or hydration (ie: feeding tubes) to keep you alive if your condition is terminal and incurable or if you are in an irreversible coma or persistent vegetative state.
- That you know your living will allow your doctor to withhold or stop extraordinary medical treatment or artificial nutrition or hydration.

Do I need witnesses in order for my living will to be valid?

Yes.

Two or sometimes three witnesses are the standard. The following list is people that would not make a good witness to your signature on your living will:

- Someone related to either you or your spouse.
- Someone who will inherit property from you
- Your doctor or any of their staff
- Someone who has a claim against you.

Honestly, it would seem the less you know the witnesses the better.

Should I have my living will to be notarized?

Yes.

To Whom do I provide a copy of my living will?

You don't have to supply the document to anyone. It's best, though, to provide a copy for your physician, your health care surrogate and other trusted individuals (ie: your spouse). The important point is to make sure someone knows where it is.

Can I change my mind? Can I revoke my living will?

Yes & yes. You can revoke your living will by informing your doctor of the change. You should do this in writing and send the notification by certified mail. Destroying the original and all copies of your living will would also be prudent.

Congratulations, you've cooked another asset!

Here's a financial diet tip!

Be careful of committing to an interest-only mortgage.

If home values decrease, you may become "upside down" on your house   purchase. You may owe more on the home than you would receive if you had to sell it.

If interest rates increase most likely so will your monthly payment.

Tiramisu Trusts
"Creating a Trust"

> If you set up an irrevocable trust for the benefit of "Little Sammy" you better be sure you'll still like "Little Sammy" ten years down the road because once you name a beneficiary of a irrevocable trust you can't change your mind. You're stuck with your decision!

Trusts? Living trusts, testamentary trusts, charitable remainder trusts, by-pass trusts, credit shelter trusts, grantor trusts are all different types of trusts. Seems like there are as many types of trusts these days as there are types of coffee drinks. Cappacino, caffe mocha, caffe latte, iced caffe mocha, iced chai latte, espresso... okay, coffee drinks win out but trusts comes in as a close second. Certain types of trusts can be very complex and confusing. This recipe will focus on using basic trust ingredients. If you want to try cooking more complicated trust recipes, seek out an attorney who specializes in estate planning.

Tiramisu Trusts
Creating a Trust

Ingredients

Grantor, trustor, settlor - person creating the trust

Trustee - one who takes care of the trust's assets

Beneficiary - person(s) who receive benefit from the trust

The trust agreement - the legal document that spells out what property is in the trust and who will be the beneficiaries.

Estate planning attorney to execute the paperwork

Preparation

1   Decide what property you want to be held in the trust. Make a schedule of the assets you choose.

2   Change the ownership registration on whatever property you put into the trust ie: a bank account in the name of The Financial Chef would be re-titled to The Financial Chef Trust

3   Decide who will benefit from the trust. These are the beneficiaries.

4   Decide who will take care of the trust 's assets, make sure tax returns are filed and distribute trust income. This person is called the trustee. It can be a lawyer, banker, you, a relative etc.

5   Have your estate planning attorney draft the trust document.

6   Place the assets in the trust.

7   Create a pour-over will to send any remaining assets not in your trust into the trust at your death so the trust remains valid and enforceable and probate is avoided.

Recipe's Financial Nutritional Value
20=Degree of Risk
30=Long Tem Value or Growth Potential
20=Income Producing
0-50=Tax Savings (depending on the trust)

Sample Portion of Change
of Beneficiary Form

> A living trust is best created by a financial/legal professional based upon your wishes. Think of it as a restaurant recipe that you can't make at home. There are just some meals that taste better when dining out then when you make them at home.

POLICY NO. _____ INSURED _____

OWNER *(If other than Insured)* _____

☐ **TRANSFER OF OWNERSHIP** - I hereby assign all my right, title and interest of said policy to the new owner designated below and vest in the new owner all incidents of ownership and the right to exercise all rights and privileges without my consent.

PRINT FULL NAME OF NEW OWNER _____ SIGNATURE OF NEW OWNER _____

ADDRESS OF NEW OWNER _____ RELATIONSHIP TO INSURED _____ AGE _____

CITY _____ STATE _____ ZIP CODE _____ SOCIAL SECURITY NO. OR TAX ID NO. OF NEW OWNER _____

☐ **CONTINGENT OWNER** - I hereby revoke the existing contingent ownership designation and designate the person named below as contingent owner. The contingent owner will become the new owner in the event the owner does not survive the Insured. If a new owner is designated, then, any prior designation of a contingent owner will be automatically voided.

PRINT FULL NAME _____ RELATIONSHIP TO INSURED _____ AGE _____

☐ **CHANGE OF BENEFICIARY**

☐ FIRST BENEFICIARY - I hereby revoke the existing designation and settlement election if any, and request that the first beneficiary designation under the above policy

> You should name a contingent beneficiary to alleviate any potential problems, should the first beneficiary die. The contingent beneficiary takes the place of the first beneficiary in this case. Sounds just like the Miss America contest!

RELATIONSHIP TO:

PRINT FULL NAME _____
ADDRESS _____
SOCIAL SECURITY NO. _____ *(If other than Insured)*

PRINT FULL NAME _____
ADDRESS _____
SOCIAL SECURITY NO. _____ *(If other than Insured)*

☐ CONTINGENT BENEFICIARY - I hereby revoke the existing contingent beneficiary designation and settlement election, if any, and request that the contingent beneficiary designation under the above policy be changed as follows:

RELATIONSHIP TO:

PRINT FULL NAME _____ INSURED _____
ADDRESS _____ OWNER _____
SOCIAL SECURITY NO. _____ DATE OF BIRTH _____ *(If other than Insured)*

PRINT FULL NAME _____ INSURED _____
ADDRESS _____ OWNER _____
SOCIAL SECURITY NO. _____ DATE OF BIRTH _____ *(If other than Insured)*

☐ Include as ☐ First ☐ Contingent beneficiary all future children of Insured's present marriage.
☐ Proceeds are **NOT** to be paid in one sum. Attach instructions for method of payment.

It is understood and agreed that, unless otherwise directed, proceeds will be paid in equal shares to any first beneficiaries who survive the Insured, but if none survives, proceeds will be paid in equal shares to any contingent beneficiaries who survive the Insured.

↓ COMPLETE FOR ABOVE REQUEST ↓

SIGNATURE OF OWNER _____ DATE _____

SIGNATURE OF NEW OWNER *(Needed if Ownership & Beneficiary Designation are being Changed)* _____ SIGNATURE OF SPOUSE IF RESIDENT OF COMMUNITY PROPERTY STATE _____

> Living trusts come in many different "shapes and sizes". This is why I'm not showing the finished product picture of a living trust. The document is better created by the professionals and as such is too long and wordy to present here. Instead, I'm presenting a change in beneficiary of the trust form. After all, what if you get mad at your cousin Betty? You'll want to know how to get rid of her!

a licensed third-party administrator

Let's talk trusts...

Why would you want to go through the hassle of setting up a trust? The primary reason is to avoid probate and the cost of probate after your death. Yes, it costs money to die. Forget the funeral costs for right now.

What are probate costs? Appraisal costs, executor's fees, legal fees, court costs and accounting fees comprise probate costs. In total, probate costs can be significant. Also, probate costs must be paid first before any assets are distributed to the beneficiaries of your estate. Furthermore, with a trust, making distributions of your estate's assets by the trustee generally happens faster than if the assets are distributed through probating the will.

Are trusts and wills the same thing? No, trusts and wills have different functions. A recipe for "White Chocolate Cheesecake Wills" presented later will clarify a will's purpose.

So what is a trust? Let me try to answer in a way that is understandable, simple and not filled with lifeless legal jargon. This would not be the answer you'd give if you were taking a test or if asked in a job interview.

A trust is a legal document created to house all your assets (real estate, stocks, money, insurance policies) under one roof. The trust is updated for additions and deletions of your assets. When you pass away, the value of all the assets in the trust is determined. This amount is excluded from probate, and the assets can be given to the listed beneficiaries.

There's that probate word again. Think of probate as a process of identifying, verifying, and distributing a deceased person's assets after the fact. Since no accounting for or verification of these assets was done prior to the person's death, all sorts of professional people that charge large fees get involved to make sure the process is done right. Whereas, keeping a trust is a process too, but the work is done before the person dies. The assets are continuously accounted for and verified. "Wow!" you're thinking. "I'm going to get a trust and avoid those fees". Hold on there a minute...With a trust, you continually pay fees throughout the life of the trust. Which is worse? Pay now or pay later. I know some of you are thinking "Pay later; since I'll be dead, I won't care? " The real answer depends on the size of your estate, the state in which you reside and at what rates do all those professionals charge.

Now, let's think of a trust as a big social party. For parties like these, the host often caters the event for their guests. A trust operates the same way as a catered affair.

Grantor – is the host of the party. They give the trust its assets. Other names used for grantor are trustor or settler. The grantor is the creator of the trust. Just like the host, they sponsor the event.

Trustee - is the caterer of the party. They administer the trust. Trustees are responsible for controlling the property in the trust, managing the trust investments, and overseeing payments and distributions. Just like the caterer, they run the show and make the event happen.

Beneficiaries – are the guests. They receive the benefits of the trust according to the terms of trust document. Just like the guests, they get to have all the fun and none of the work or responsibility.

Trusts that are created during the grantors lifetime are called living trusts or *inter vivos* trust. A trust created by the grantor's will is called a testamentary trust.

Often living trusts "turn into" testamentary trusts upon the grantor's death. There is paperwork that occurs behind the scenes to enable this transition to flow so well.

Trusts that allow you to modify its terms are called revocable trusts. Trusts that don't allow you to change its terms once it has been established are called irrevocable trusts.

Some of the best candidates for a living trust:

- Those with a greater risk of death – older/unhealthy individuals. Younger, healthy people with few assets probably don't need a living trust now.
- Those with significant assets, especially if those assets include real estate.

With a revocable trust, you, as grantor, retain control over the property that is placed in the trust. You can change trustees and beneficiaries at any time. However,when you die, the beneficiaries and trustees you have named become fixed and permanent.

Many people think starting a revocable trust will save them taxes each year. This is not the case. Basically, with a revocable trust, you still own the assets in the trust. The IRS loves to tax things we own. Instead, revocable or living trusts are best used for avoiding probate.

If a revocable trust gives you flexibility, you can be assured that someone created the opposite type or an irrevocable trust. An irrevocable trust cannot be amended, revoked, terminated or changed by the grantor or anyone else once it becomes effective. With an irrevocable trust, you are giving up all your rights to the property you place in the trust.

Why would you want to do that? Since you no longer own the assets that are placed in your irrevocable trust, when you die these assets will not be part of your estate. If the assets are excluded from your estate, you may escape some estate tax.

Now, I have to get a little complicated for a minute. When you put assets into an irrevocable trust, the IRS thinks you made a gift. Some gifts, if large enough, can be subject to a gift tax.

So some assets are better than others to put into an irrevocable trust. Which are better? Assets that will appreciate over time are one good candidate. For example, if you own a piece of property that's not valuable now but you really think its worth will appreciate in the future, you should place it in the trust. From a gift tax standpoint, the value is low so the transfer of the property to an irrevocable trust is tax-free. Now, here's the good part. As the property appreciates in value is does so tax-free. So when you die, the transfer of the irrevocable trust property to your beneficiary(s) is estate not taxed.

So assets that will grow in value in the future are good choices for an irrevocable trust.

Another good asset choice for an irrevocable trust is life insurance. If life insurance is transferred into an irrevocable trust, the proceeds payable upon your death pass to your beneficiaries without any estate taxes charged. So you could purchase a ten million dollar life insurance policy, fund it to an irrevocable trust, pay the premiums from the irrevocable trust and not pay a dime of estate taxes on the proceeds when you die. Not that anyone can really afford a ten million dollar life insurance policy, but you get the idea.

I used a term in the previous paragraph "fund the trust". This concept is important.

Once created, the trust must be "funded". The funding of a trust is the process of transferring the assets from your own name to the trust's name. Deeds to real property must be prepared and recorded in the trust name. Your attorney will do this for you. Bank accounts and stock or bond certificates need to be transferred as well. These tasks are not extremely complicated but necessary to make your trust valid. Much time and paperwork will be needed to complete the process.

Here are some of the advantages and disadvantages of establishing a revocable living trust:

Advantages

- Avoidance of probate costs – and also faster distribution of your estate's assets when funded in a living trust.
- Privacy protection – those assets in a living trust are not of public record. A will becomes part ofpublic record. The size of your estate, the beneficiaries and the amounts each received will be available to anyone.
- Unifying real estate holdings -Those with real estate holdings in multiple states will avoid potential problems of multiple probate proceedings by "putting all their eggs in on living trust basket. "
- Protection for minor children – a living trust can be used to control a guardian's actions if he/she is acting on behalf of minor children. A trust can stipulate conditions that have to be met in order for distributions to be made.

Disadvantages

- Re-titling the property - This can be a time consuming hassle. There also may be some fees associated with re-titling.
- Administrative fees- If you appoint a bank or a trust company to act as trustee, it will charge you fees. You must also keep books and records of all the trust assets and their activity, which may also cost you fees besides the additional time factor.
- Cost to create the trust document -This cost varies with the complexity of the trust. Retaining an attorney to draw up the documents is advisable and usually doesn't come cheap.

I'd like to wrap this recipe up with one final note. This is a repetitive point, so it must be really important. If you choose to establish a revocable or irrevocable trust, please do not be remiss in funding the trust.

I saw a situation where a couple created two irrevocable trusts to hold two $5,000,000 life insurance policies for their beneficiaries. A very unfortunate car accident occurred killing them both. Since the life insurance policies were never "re-titled" to the trust nor were the premiums paid from the trust, the entire ten million dollars of life insurance proceeds became part of their estate and subject to estate tax rules. At tax rates hovering in the 40% range, that's a big mistake. Uncle Sam became the major beneficiary to this couple's estate rather than their children. If they had properly funded the irrevocable trust, the ten million would have passed to their children completely tax- free. So please, if you create a trust don't forget to "fund" it.

Congratulations! You've cooked another asset!

Flan Funeral Plans

"Making a Funeral Plan"

Misplacing the deceased, moving grave sites, embezzling funds have put funeral homes in a bad light recently. Due to these scams, the government has stepped in and added strict regulatory conditions for funeral homes. These measures should provide the consumer more trust when making funeral arrangements

You are your biggest asset! And your last mark in this lifetime will be your funeral. Now stop thinking what do I care? I'll be dead. You should be thinking about your family and friends. Number one, do not leave your family with the bill for your funeral. Second, try to put into place a framework of how you would like your funeral to be. Pre-paying and pre-planning your funeral will save your family and friends a lot of stress.

Flan Funeral Plans

"Making a Funeral Plan"

Ingredients

The deceased

A funeral service candidate (arranger)—you, spouse, family member

A funeral home

A budget for the cost of the service (money)

Either a funeral trust or a funeral insurance policy

Copy of the pre-need contract with the funeral home detailing the pre-paid services. Make sure your loved ones know where this contract is stored.

Preparation

1. *Meet with a few funeral directors to inquire what they offer for prepaid funeral plans. Be aware that state regulations differ, so funeral director's services will vary according to their applicable state law.*

2. *Funeral director will provide a Statement of Funeral Goods and Services which describes the exact goods and services you are purchasing.*

3. *Complete the prepaid agreement which outlines the terms and conditions of the agreement including the amount of money paid and where the money will be deposited. This will be either in an interest bearing trust account or funded in a funeral insurance policy.*

4. *Make copies of the agreement. Store a copy in your safe deposit box and provide another copy to your will's named personal representative.*

Recipe's Financial Nutritional Value
20=Degree of Risk
20=Long Tem Value or Growth Potential
20=Income Producing
0=Tax Savings

Sample Funeral General Price List

Funerals "R" Us
555 Main Street
Anywhere, USA 55555

Sample General Price List

Deceased:_____

Purchaser:_____

Address:_____

Date of Death_____

Date of Arrangements:_____

Basic Services of Funeral Director and Staff including Overhead $_____

Embalming $_____

  Except in certain special cases, embalming is not required by law. Embalming may be necessary depending on the type of funeral service you have requested. There are burial services such as direct cremation or immediate burial that often do not require embalming.

Other Preparation of the Body $_____
  Topical Disinfections $_____
  Custodial Care charge per day $_____
  Cosmetic Care $_____
  Dressing/ Casketing $_____
  Restoration $_____

Transfer of Remains to the Funeral Home $_____

Viewing Funeral Expenses $_____

Funeral Ceremony Expenses $_____

Memorial Service Expenses $_____

Graveside Service Expenses $_____

Hearse/Limousine Expenses $_____

Casket $_____

Funerals "R" Us
555 Main Street
Anywhere, USA 55555

Sample General Price List

Alternative Containers $_____

Forwarding of Remains to Another Funeral Home $_____

Receiving of Remains from Another Funeral Home $_____

Cash Advances
Cemetery Charges $_____
Clergy Honorarium $_____
Certified Copies of Death Certificates $_____

Need more funeral planning information...

I've had to arrange a few funerals for loved ones myself. It's not an easy task, especially if you haven't received any assistance from the departed. Do they want to be cremated or have a burial? What type of casket? What type of urn? Will there be a visitation? Will it be open or closed casket? These are just a few decisions to be resolved. What makes planning so difficult is the realization that you can't ask the deceased what their wishes are. To make matters worse, scores of other relatives (appearing out of no where) will offer their ideas, pulling you in a hundred different directions.

Funerals are expensive. Making provisions yourself ahead of time, reduces the financial and emotional stress that may be placed on your loved ones later. Many funeral homes offer funeral plans that are either guaranteed or non-guaranteed funerals.

Some funeral directors provide a guarantee that the prices charged for the funeral's goods and services will not increase or be subject to inflation. This is great for the consumer because the guarantee locks in the price at current rates for services that will be rendered in the future. How often have you seen the price of an item go down in the future? A plasma television is about the only thing I can think of. Funeral directors can also elect not to provide price guarantees. If you take this option, be aware what you've prepaid probably won't be sufficient to cover your entire future funeral costs. This leaves your loved ones with the decision of spending more money or cutting back on services performed.

I don't know about you, but here's my thinking. I'm dead. My funeral is the last time people are going to see me and I want to look great. If I don't prepay for my funeral, my relatives will decide if it's necessary to give me makeup or a great hairstyle or a cool outfit. No makeup? I don't even go to the grocery store without makeup. I certainly would want to start the natural look at my funeral.

In fairness to your family, today's $40 pedicure could be $300 by the time you die. That's a lot of money for pretty feet. So I say, if you think you'll want it later, you better pay for it now!

Whether you select the guaranteed or non-guaranteed alternative, it must be disclosed in writing at the time you are making the arrangements.

Many states offer these two methods of funding your pre-paid plan. You can choose a funeral trust or a funeral insurance policy. A funeral trust can be set up at bank or with a local funeral home. Funeral trusts should be funded in interest bearing accounts. The funeral director should not commingle the trust funds with their regular operating funds.

Funeral insurance policies only cover funeral expenses. The proceeds can not be used for non-related funeral expenses. At the time of death, the face value of the policy is paid to the policy's beneficiary. The beneficiary can be the funeral home or a designated third party that will have to pay the funeral home. If you do name the funeral home as the beneficiary, make sure that you have the option to change the beneficiary in the future should you decide to move or change funeral homes. Also, ask the funeral director if he or she is receiving a commission on the policy.

Misplacing the deceased, moving grave sites, and embezzling prepaid funeral funds have cast a dark cloud over the funeral home industry. Regulations have stiffened in an effort to provide consumers with additional security. Here are a few follow up steps to make certain that you prepaid funds are being handled correctly.

- If you have established funeral insurance, make sure you physically receive a copy of the policy and that you review its terms.
- If you have established funeral trust, verify that your funds are part of the trust's bank account. You can do this by contacting the financial institution holding the funds and asking for receipt of your funds.
- Request two referrals of customers that have used the funeral home's services in the last three months. Contact the parties and ask them if they were satisfied with their funerals.
- Look for state licenses posted in the funeral home.

The next section although ancillary to the vital issue of pre-funding your funeral costs, is presented to help those who will plan funerals for others. From my experience, I found myself guessing what the wishes were of my family member that had passed away. Here are some concerns I faced :

➢ Where should the funeral take place?

Sounds like an easy question, but is it really? Your mom was married to your dad for thirty years. He flies a few too many times on United Airlines, if you know what I mean. Your mom's divorced now. Unfortunately, she's dies in a terrible accident. You have to take care of her funeral arrangements. Years ago, she and your dad purchased cemetery plots next to each other. You bury your mom in the plot next to the plot reserved for your dad. Big mistake. Your dad's new wife is livid with you. Your mom? Well, she literally is rolling over in her grave because she wants out or at least away from your dad.

➢ Who will be the clergy presiding over the service?

Often, this is an issue that has family members, you rarely see or hear from, appear from nowhere and insist on using their candidates.

➢ Will there be memorial contributions?

 Donated flowers will always be a part of funeral service. The deceased may also designate an organization that they wish to receive any cash donations. Often, this is the association trying to find a cure for the illness that defeated the deceased. Frequently, these groups are not-for-profit and volunteer based. Asking for cash pledges to charities in lieu of flowers is a personal choice. If you like the idea, make sure you let someone know what your cause is before it's too late.

➢ What will the music be?

Personally, I wouldn't really care what music is played. For others... well... anything can be a source of controversy. What can I say?

➢ Will there be a viewing? If so, what will be the clothing?

I think common sense needs to be used when answering this question. It is a personal preference of the deceased if they would want a viewing. For many, a viewing provides an opportunity to say goodbye and to get some closure. However, this being said, I think the cause of death and the condition of the body should be a strong consideration when determining if a viewing is appropriate.

Okay, so here's a hypothetical situation. Julie passes away. Her relatives all agree on a viewing. Her husband, Jack, is responsible for choosing her final funeral outfit. Julie left her last fashion statement in the hands of a tee shirt and ripped jeans kind of guy. Julie wore a black mid-calf wool skirt with a black polyester blouse and black flat ballet flats. Where's the color? Well, Jack thought, it's a funeral, she has to wear black. Julie can't believe her eternity will be spent looking like a depressed schoolteacher (You're thinking, "She's dead. What will she know? " Remember, I did say this is a hypothetical situation) Point of the story is this. Although, it may seem morbid, making some of these choices ahead of time may bring you some peace of mind during your lifetime.

➢ **Should there be a spiritual message on the funeral invitation?**

Again, if this is important to you, please give your message to someone ahead of time.

➢ **What type of flowers would the deceased have liked?**

This too is a personal decision. My sister and I spent a lot of time at the florist trying to decide what flowers my dad would like for his funeral. Finally, we decided on a lottery ticket flower arrangement. We chose a unique bunch of wild flowers with ten lottery tickets nestled in the greens. An avid player, believing he could mathematically beat the lottery system, I'm sure my dad loved the display.

Although the answers to the above questions are more personal than economical, they are still important because they are a reflection of you. Your funeral is your final opportunity to be heard by those who care about you.

Congratulations! You've cooked another asset!

White Chocolate Cheesecake Wills

"Drafting a Last Will and Testament"

Not having your own last will and testament is like being arrested and not having your own lawyer. The State will assign you a will if you die just like they will assign you a public defender if you're arrested. No offense to all you public defenders but I wouldn't want to leave such important matters in control of the government!

Picture this. A few years back, your wonderful husband gives you an awesome diamond tennis bracelet for Christmas. You absolutely love it and receive many compliments on how brilliant it is. Your sister especially admires the bracelet. You have a semi-morbid thought, that if you die, your sister Sally should get the bracelet. Well, something bad does happen to you; you die. Freak accident. You have no will. Your husband oblivious to your semi-morbid thought, gives your diamond tennis bracelet to his mother! How could he? Certainly, he knew that Sally's wrist was far more delicate and dainty then his mother's... Well, lets not go there. I think you get the idea.

Moral of the story— Make sure you have a will.

White Chocolate Cheesecake Wills

"Drafting a Last Will and Testament"

Ingredients

Your estate

Your attorney

Beneficiaries

Executor

Last will and testament document

Witnesses (optional)

Preparation

1. *Create an inventory of your assets and liabilities placing a reasonable value on each item.*
2. *Decide who you want to be your personal representative or executor. This is the person that will of carry out your will's objectives.*
3. *Choose which people you want to receive your assets. These people are called your beneficiaries.*
4. *Hire an attorney to draft the Last Will and Testament document.*
5. *Once drafted read through the entire will and make sure you understand everything it states.*
6. *Have two independent people witness your signature on the will.*
7. *Revise and update your will for life changes.*

Recipe's Financial Nutritional Value
20=Degree of Risk
 0=Long Tem Value or Growth Potential
10=Income Producing
20=Tax Savings

Sample Portion Last Will and Testament

LAST WILL AND TESTAMENT
OF
_____ [name]

I, _____ [name], residing at _____ [address], do hereby make, publish and declare this to be my Last Will and Testament and hereby revoke any and all Wills and Codicils at any time heretofore made by me.

FIRST: I declare that I am not married and have no children.

SECOND: I direct that the expenses of my funeral and burial [or cremation] be paid out of my estate in such amount as my Personal Representative may deem proper and without regard to any limitation in the applicable law or rule of court as to the amount of such expenses and without the necessity of court approval.

I direct that (a) all estate, inheritance, succession and other death taxes and duties occasioned by my death, whether incurred with respect to property passing by this Will or otherwise, but excluding any generation-skipping tax, and (b) all cost of packing, shipping, insurance and other charges incidental to the distribution of any tangible personal property herein, shall be paid by my Personal Representative out of the principal of my residuary estate (as hereinafter defined) with no right of reimbursement from any recipient of such property.

THIRD: I hereby confirm my intention that the beneficial interest in all property, real or personal, tangible or intangible (including joint checking or saving accounts in any bank or savings and loan association or credit union), which is registered or held, at the time of my death, jointly in the names of myself and any other person (including tenancy by the entireties, but excluding any tenancy in common), shall pass by right of survivorship or operation of law and outside the terms of this Will to such other person if he or she survives me. To the extent that my intention may be defeated by any rule of law, I give or devise and bequeath all such jointly held property to such other person or persons who shall survive me.

FOURTH [optional]: I give, devise and bequeath to _____
_____
[name] _____ [specifically list whom you want to leave things to and what you want to leave to them] absolutely [or in fee simple absolute] if s/he survives me.

FIFTH: I give and bequeath all of my tangible personal property, not otherwise disposed of, to _____ [name of individual] if s/he survives me. If s/he fails to survive me, I give and bequeath my tangible personal property to those of _____[names of individuals] as survive

1

me, in equal shares as they shall agree or, failing agreement, then in such a manner as my Personal Representative shall determine.

SIXTH: All the rest, residue and remainder of my property and estate, of whatever character, whensoever acquired and wheresoever situated and to which I or my estate may be in any manner entitled at the time of my death, including any property or estate as to which I may have any power of disposition or appointment and further including any request which may have lapsed due to failure of a legatee to survive me (all said property and estate being herein referred to as my "residuary estate"), shall be disposed of as follows:

I give the residuary of my estate in fee simple absolute to _____, if s/he survives me and if not, to _____.

SEVENTH: If any person who shall be
is a minor at the time distribution is to b
_____ [yo
corresponding statute of any other state v
Personal Representative to receive such
as custodian an adult, a guardian of the r
custodian shall constitute a full acquitta

> A personal representative is responsible for the settlement of your estate. It can be a very time consuming and stressful job. Be aware of what would be required before you agree to take on the task. In exchange for your services, you can charge a fee. Usually the fee is based upon a percentage of the value of the deceased's estate.

EIGHTH: I nominate and appoint _____
Representative of this my Last Will and
serve, or fail to qualify within a reasonal
nomination, I nominate and appoint _____, as his/her successor,
and I direct that neither my Personal Representative nor his/her successor be required to give bond or undertaking or security thereon in any jurisdiction.

My Personal Representative shall have full discretionary power, in addition to any powers provided by law, without order or approval of any court, to take any action desirable for administration of my estate, including the power to sell at public or private sale, any real or personal property belonging to my estate at whatever prices and upon what ever terms s/he shall deem advisable, to retain, invest or reinvest in any property without responsibility for diversification and without being restricted by any rule of law or court limiting investments, to hold securities in the name of the nominee, to compromise any claims to the same extent I could, if living, and to distribute in kind or in money or partly in each, even if shares be composed differently.

NINTH: (A) For the purposes of the Will, other than the appointment of my Personal Representative, if a legatee shall die with me in a common accident or disaster, or under such circumstances as to make it impossible or difficult to determine which of us died first or in the event that any such legatee shall die within thirty (30) full days of my death, then such legatee shall be considered to have predeceased me. This clause shall not apply in any case where its application would cause any provision of this Will, which would

2

otherwise be valid, to be void under any applicable rule against perpetuities, rule limiting suspension of the power of alienation or other similar rule.

(B) No successor Personal Representative under this Will shall be liable for any act or omission of a predecessor Personal Representative nor shall s/he be obliged to inquire into the validity or propriety of any such act or omission by his or her predecessor. Any such successor Personal Representative shall be entitled to accept as conclusive any accounting and statement of assets furnished to such successor by his or her predecessor, and shall further be entitled to receipt only for those assets included in such statement.

In Witness Whereof, I have set my hand to this my Last Will and Testament and on the bottom of each of the preceding _____ and the following ___ pages I have affixed my signature for better identification this _____ day of _____, 20_____.

_____
[signature]

Important Note: This sample legal document is provided for informational purposes only and may or may not be valid in your particular state. This sample legal document also may not include the particular provisions you need. We strongly recommend that you consult a competent family or estate planning attorney who is familiar with these issues. This sample legal document in no way constitutes, and should not be relied upon, as legal advice.

Want more information on drafting a will...

Everyone has heard the expression "You can't take it with you when you die. " So what happens to "It" then? And what is "It"? The "It" is your estate, which is equal to the balance of all your assets minus all your debts. What happens to "It" depends on if you have executed a will.

If you die without a will, you have died intestate. The laws of the state in which you reside control the distribution of your assets. It may mean the following:

❖ Instead of giving your entire estate to your spouse, the state may give your spouse only one third of your estate with the other two thirds going directly to your children.

❖ If both you and your spouse die without a will and your children are minors, the state may decide who will be your children's guardian regardless of your wishes.

❖ Your specific bequests may not be honored. You wanted the "antique necklace" that had been in your family for years to be given to your niece Samantha. If an unsolvable family feud breaks out over who will get the necklace, the court will have the necklace sold andthe proceeds divided.

Here's a more cynical example. You're single. You saved your money to take a trip to Japan. While there you stumble upon a stunning silk kimono. It is one of a kind, but very expensive. Throwing caution to the wind, you purchase it. When you arrive home, you show it to your mother who also falls in love with the kimono. You tell your mother that if anything ever should happen to you , you want her to have the kimono.

Something does happen to you. You die. Freak accident (damn those freak accidents). You have no will. Your black sheep of the family sister goes over to your apartment and takes the kimono. Your mother finds out that your sister has been wearing the kimono. She demands the kimono, stating that you had wanted her to have it. Your sister states that you bought the kimono as a belated birthday present for her.

Without a will, your intentions are not legally known or documented. Your mother can't prove that you had wanted her to have the robe. Your sister stole your treasure and will not be caught. Whew, pretty cold example.

Okay, so now you see that having a will is a good thing. Should one draft her own will or have an attorney do the job? If you can afford the fee, have a lawyer draft the document.

What provisions do most wills contain?

- ❖ Your name as Testator (this is why if you die without a will, the term is intestate)
- ❖ Your spouse's name if applicable
- ❖ Your children's names if applicable
- ❖ Who you want to the personal representative (executor, administrator) of your estate
- ❖ A statement that this will revokes any other prior wills
- ❖ Any specific gifts or bequests
- ❖ How the remainder of your assets (after paying all your liabilities) will be distributed

Some have asked " Can I disinherit my spouse? "

The answer is "Not completely", unless your spouse signed a prenuptial agreement releasing any rights to your estate upon your death. And who would sign off on that? Also, each state has its own laws that frown upon completely cutting off your spouse. Personally, why would you be thinking like that anyway? If you are, you may want to consider a divorce, also.

It would only make sense that the next question be, "Can I disinherit my child? "

The answer is "Generally, yes. "If the child is a minor, the state will make you provide an allowance to support the child, as a rule, until he reaches the age of 18. Otherwise, if you want to cut off one or all of your children in your will, you need to make a statement referencing that the omission is intentional.

Drafting a will can get pretty ugly.

What about divorce? Does that destroy the validity of my will. The answer depends upon the state that in which you reside. In some states, the will is automatically revoked upon divorce. In other states, just the sections that pertain to your ex-spouse are voided. In any case, after a divorce, revise your will to adjust for this large life- changing event.

One day, hopefully much later than sooner, you will die. You've been smart and executed a will. "Wait," you think. "I'm not going to be around anymore to carry out the will's instructions. Who's going to do it? "To minimize any confusion and potential arguments, you should name an executor or personal representative to handle the affairs of your estate.

The personal representative doesn't have to do all the work himself. He can hire a lawyer and accountant to help with the tasks but still he oversees the whole process. You will want to name alternate executors in case your primary choice is unwilling or unable to act.

Now, I'll be frank. This is my personal opinion, so take it for what it's worth. Being a personal representative is a necessary evil that you do for someone out of the kindness of your heart. It is a pretty ungrateful job, speaking from experience. It does pay but.... But it is also a very important job, and your candidate should be trustworthy and competent. It wouldn't hurt if he also had some business sense.

Suppose a few years go by from when you executed your will. When you first drafted it, you were very fond of your sister-in-law Cheryl. Since then Cheryl has cheated on your brother, and, although he may have forgiven her, you haven't. You want to change your will. You have two choices. You can either prepare and execute a new will that revokes this earlier will, or you can add a codicil to the will (like an addendum) that contains the new changes. Your attorney will help you make the best choice.

Besides having a falling out with one of the beneficiaries of your will, there are other times that you may want to update your will. They are:

- Getting married.
- Getting divorced.
- Having a child.
- Death of a beneficiary or family member.
- Substantial changes in the value of your estate.

Also in this category are considerable changes in the types of assets in your estate. For example,you owned a large boat when you first drafted your will and bequeath it to your daredevil brother, Ricky. Since then you've tired of the boat and sold it in exchange for an investment in rare stamps. You don't think Ricky will be into a stamp collection, so you want to update your will. Stamps are more your cousin, Melvin's speed.

- You're moving to another state. As I've mentioned throughout this recipe, each state has its own rules when it comes to wills. Find a new attorney in your new state.
- Your children are old enough and don't need a guardian.

Congratulations, you've cooked another asset!

Epilogue – Menu Makeovers

Whew! We've been busy. We've discussed a bunch of personal finance recipes. Each recipe with its own set of ingredients and steps for preparation. You're probably a bit overwhelmed right now. You may be thinking "Which recipe should I prepare first? Can I make more than one recipe to create an entire meal?" Both are great questions.

First, let me say, that there isn't one specific recipe that everyone should make first. Each individual's circumstances differ. What may be a great starter recipe for one person may make no sense for someone else. For instance, a couple who owns a home might opt to prepare *Refinanced Mortgage with Ranchero Sauce*. Interest rates move low enough making the timing perfect for them to refinance. This recipe wouldn't be a good choice for Tyler, though. He doesn't own a home; instead he just started his first real job. He wants to tuck some money away in a retirement fund, but his company doesn't sponsor any pension plans. A good starter recipe for Tyler might be *IRA Imperial.*

Creating an entire meal takes a little more thought and planning. There are recipes combinations that are meant to be paired. Beans and franks, or fish and chips, or sausage and peppers, or peanut butter and jelly are combos that have survived through the ages. Yet, there are more recipe combinations that don't work than those that do. Creating a meal can be tricky.

Let's invite back Risky Rick, Moderate Melvin, Conservative Clara and Debtor Debbie and show how we can makeover their meal plans.

Starting with Risky Rick, let's look at some of his favorite recipes:

o IPOs (Initial Public Offerings) Orzo
o Variable Rate Mortgage Vinaigrette
o Filet of "Flip This House" Investments
o Pesto Penny Stock Purchases
o Oil and Gas Investments Oreganato

Risky Rick makes these recipes all the time. I can't figure out why though. He's always complaining that whenever he makes one of these recipes, it doesn't turn out like he planned.

He needs to mix up his menu choices. Too much risk isn't good for his financial diet. He needs to prepare more of the financial chef's recipes. He can still add an occasional risky recipe but only as a side dish.

Here are a few recipes that would help Risky Rick have a more balanced diet:

Bistro Bruschetta Budgets (to try to rein in his spontaneous investments),Decadent Disability Insurance (Risky Rick is an avid skier and sky diver) and Refinanced Mortgage with Ranchero Sauce (to take the place of his Variable Rate Mortgage Vinaigrette Recipe).

Next up is Moderate Melvin. Here are some of his favorite recipes.

o   Mesquite Grilled Money Market Accounts
o   Chili-Cheese Certificates of Deposits
o   Roasted Garlic Rental Apartment

He needs to commit to some long- term investments. He's rented an apartment for years and not because he doesn't have enough money for the down payment. Moderate Melvin just doesn't want the responsibility of a owning a house.

Well, Moderate Melvin, grow up! If the housing market is good in your neighborhood, start looking Melvin.

Moderate Melvin needs some spice in his diet. His recipes are bland, although they sound tasty. He should at least become familiar with the recipes for House Purchase with Hollandaise, Garlic Mashed Mortgages and Honey Glazed Home Insurance. If he searches hard enough, he may find a great deal, even when the real estate market is down. Another recipe he should make part of his inventory is Iron Skillet Investments. He should branch out from the everyday Mesquite Grilled Money Markets Accounts and take on additional risk.

Now let's check out Conservative Clara. Actually, there's really not too much to review. She's limited herself to a few recipes.

o   Checking Accounts With Crispy Cash
o   Bistro Bruschetta Budgets
o   Tempura Taxes
o   Caribbean Coupon Clipping

She has a checking account. She lives, eats and breathes by her budget. She also prepares her own tax return. There's not much to the tax return. Conservative Clara doesn't own anything. . She's got a good stash of cash but doesn't have any other investments. Some would say "Hey, having a lot of cash is a good thing! She's got the right idea. " Well, there is some truth to this statement. Being in Conservative Clara's position certainly would be better than having no assets at all.

Even so, Conservative Clara needs to have her money work better for her. She can accomplish this by introducing acceptable amounts of risk in her life.

She needs to embrace the idea of risk, not only from a financial standpoint but from a personal stance too. Conservative Clara is rigid with not just her finances but also her life style. She's thirty-four years old and still lives at home! This certainly doesn't do much for her dating life. She's conservative with her job choice, her clothes, and her appearance. Honestly, not to be rude, Conservative Clara, you're not just conservative but you're rather cheap. She hoards mustard, ketchup, and salt and pepper packets from fast food restaurants. She re-gifts presents she doesn't like. Investing her stashed cash for a profit may be enough for Conservative Clara to break free of her penny-pinching practices.

If Conservative Clara adds some recipes with risk to her diet, she might loosen up a little. She may even buy a wild leopard print cocktail dress and go out on a date.

Here are a few recipes that will help her open new financial doors:

Creamy Chipolte Credit Card Dip (for emergencies and to establish credit for the future), Iron Skillet Investments (to earn both interest and dividends) and IRA Imperial (to earn tax free money tax for the long term).

Our final makeover candidate is Debtor Debbie. Comparing all four subjects, I believe, Debtor Debbie's actions are the most self-destructive. She is a sub-prime loan addict. What is sub prime loan? Basically, it is financing that charges higher than normal interest rates because the borrower has issues. These issues can be bad credit, little equity (i. e. : down payment) or questionable income to repay the loan. The sub-prime virus has affected auto loans, housing loans and credit cards.

Debtor Debbie doesn't think she has a problem. So I gave her a little debt dodging reality quiz: See how you score.

Have You Ever Thought Like This or Done Any of These?

❖ Applied for a new credit card so you could pay the monthly balance of an existing one?

❖ Pretended to be someone else when answering a past due collection call?

❖ Thrown out your bills just because you didn't want to pay them?

❖ Purposely wrote the wrong payee to pay a bill just to bide more time?

❖ Convinced yourself that you're so far in debt now, what difference would it make to charge another item?

❖ Or actually hung up on a collection caller? ... pretending you lost the connection.

Debtor Debbie answered yes to all these questions. She failed the quiz. If you answered yes to any of these questions, you may want to take a step back and honestly review your own debt habits .

These are a few of Debtor Debbie's favorite recipes:

o Poached Payroll Advance

o Layaway Leg of Lamb

o Country-Style Collection Notice

Professional counseling may be required for Debtor Debbie if she can't control her spending or reduce her outstanding balances. A few recipes that will help her get back on track are: Coconut Encrusted Credit Reports (to face her credit score- this could be a real eye opener for her), Bistro Bruschetta Budgets (Debtor Debbie needs accountability) and perhaps Dijon Debt Consolidation (This recipe is not covered in this book but is pretty self-explanatory. Make sure you find a reputable company.)

I hope you take some time and effort to assess your financial diet. Maybe it's time for your own menu makeover. There are more financial recipes out there than those discussed in this book. This book will help you get started. I wish all the Cook Your Asset readers, the best financial health!

Index

www.ingramcontent.com/pod-product-compliance
Lightning Source LLC
Chambersburg PA
CBHW081720220526

45468CB00008B/1921